3
S TEPS
to YES

3
STEPS
to YES

The Gentle Art
of Getting
Your Way

GENE BEDELL

CROWN
BUSINESS
NEW YORK

Copyright © 2000 by Gene Bedell
All rights reserved. No part of this book may be reproduced or
transmitted in any form or by any means, electronic or mechanical,
including photocopying, recording, or by any information storage and
retrieval system, without permission in writing from the publisher.

Published by Crown Business, New York, New York.
Member of the Crown Publishing Group.

Random House, Inc. New York, Toronto, London, Sydney, Auckland
www.randomhouse.com

CROWN BUSINESS and colophon are trademarks of
Random House, Inc.

Printed in the United States of America

Design by Susan Hood

Library of Congress Cataloging-in-Publication Data
Bedell, Gene.
    3 steps to yes : the gentle art of getting your way /
by Gene Bedell. — 1st ed.
        p.   cm.
    1. Persuasion (Psychology) 2. Influence (Psychology)
3. Communication—Psychological aspects. I. Title.
BF637.P4.B34 2000
153.8′52—dc21
                                        00-031417
ISBN 0-609-60698-0

10 9 8 7 6 5 4 3 2 1

First Edition

The story's about you.

Horace

Contents

STEP 3: *Communicate Persuasively*

3
STEPS
to YES

Introduction

Why You Need This Book

I CAN UNDERSTAND YOUR WANTING TO WRITE
POEMS, BUT I DON'T QUITE KNOW WHAT YOU MEAN
BY "BEING A POET" . . .

—*T. S. Eliot*

My wife, a liberal arts major in college, took a course in her freshman year that she affectionately called Astronomy for Poets. She learned basic astronomy, studied the constellations, and viewed planets and stars for the first time through a telescope. Cool. She loved the course and signed up for the second in the series in her sophomore year.

Big mistake. The professor started the first class by announcing, "Well, now that we're all here for something beyond fulfilling the basic science requirement, we can get down to work." My wife's reaction as she looked around the room was *Uh-oh*. There were eight students in the class—six astronomy majors, one physics major, and one political science major: her. Not good. The course covered spherical trigonometry, sidereal time, parallax motion, optics, and a lot of other astronomy stuff that was of no interest or use to people not majoring in astronomy. My wife stuck it out, but broke the sound barrier getting to the registrar's office to change her status to pass-fail.

My wife's college and her Astronomy for Poets course weren't unique. Although they're listed in course catalogs with less irreverent titles, there's Physics for Poets, Chemistry for Poets, Rocks for Jocks (Introduction to Geology). "Poet" is a metaphor for "enlightened amateur," a person who wants to know something about astronomy—or physics, chemistry, or geology—but who doesn't want to get lost in the minutiae that only science majors need and love.

3 Steps to Yes is the persuasion equivalent of Astronomy for Poets. Here, "Poets" is a metaphor for people who must get others to agree with them, ordinary people who need to move others from no or maybe to yes, but who don't want to spend their lives learning and perfecting sales and negotiation strategies. Moreover, Poets must persuade gently, eschewing the coercion and manipulation that professional persuaders use, but that tend to corrode personal relationships.

In *3 Steps to Yes*, "Poets" are the enlightened amateurs of persuasion. They're managers, employees, parents, spouses, teachers, students, business executives, lawyers, accountants, consultants, investment bankers, job seekers, and, yes, even poets. They may even be people who sell for a living.

But "Poets" are *not* hard-core, high-pressure salespeople and negotiators, people who care only about winning and not about the quality of their long-term relationships with the people they persuade. Poets care about being liked and accepted, and avoid doing anything they feel might hurt their personal relationships.

Nevertheless, Poets must persuade.

THE POET PERSUADER

As this book neared completion, I needed a publicist, a professional public-relations person to help tell the world about my book. I narrowed my search to three firms, each run by a woman founder/entrepreneur. They were all strong, self-confident professionals working in the heart of the New York City publishing world, where only the most intelligent and influential succeed. So I was unprepared for their strong Poet aversion to persuading.

As it turned out, each woman disliked selling, and worked hard to appear *not* to be trying to persuade me. Each one seemed to operate on the theory that persuasion was unnecessary, even unseemly, and that if she simply described what she did, I'd automatically conclude that she was the best. But it doesn't work that way.

This was an important decision, so I met with the head of each firm personally. The women were competent, hardworking, and enthusiastic, and they were anxious for me to believe they could help me. They were intelligent, articulate professionals, perhaps even brilliant, but they Talked Without Communicating. My last meeting was typical, although also the most frustrating of the three.

I'd heard from an independent source that this person was "the best," so I went into this final meeting prepared to make a positive decision. I had a book about to be published, I needed help getting the word out, and I wanted to put this behind me. I was a soft pitch ready to be hit over the outfield fence. But it was not to be.

She refused to try to persuade me. Instead we played "Stump the Band," with me asking the questions and trying to guess why she was the best choice. At one point I asked her outright, "Why won't you just tell me why I should hire you instead of someone else? Honest, I won't think less of you if you tell me why you're better than people you clearly don't think are as good as you are."

Her response was that she didn't feel comfortable selling

herself, telling me why she was better. She knew she was the best, but *she wanted me to figure it out for myself based on her objective presentation of facts.* All three women, though, told me nearly the same facts about their firms: "We work hard for our clients." "All our clients come to us through word-of-mouth recommendations." "We're well connected with the print, radio, and TV media." "We have an impressive list of successful and satisfied clients." I couldn't distinguish among the different stories and capabilities, because all said essentially the same good and impressive things.

Even the woman I was predisposed to choose didn't give me what I needed to make a decision. She was not persuasive. If I were to make a decision based on the three meetings, I might just as well have flipped a coin.

SELL YOURSELF

These three women were Poets who needed to sell in the classic sense, to get someone to pay money for their services. But you don't have to be a CEO or a professional salesperson to have to sell yourself, your ideas, or your services.

In everyday life, a Poet can be a parent persuading a child to drive sensibly or avoid drugs, or a caring son or daughter persuading an elderly parent to move to a nursing home. A Poet can be a manager persuading a boss to approve her budget or an employee to work over the weekend; a job candidate persuading an interviewer about his qualifications; a lawyer, accountant, or other professional persuading a client; or a wife persuading her husband to vacation trekking in Maine instead of visiting his old college roommate in Minnesota.

For Poets, persuasion is serious life stuff. *The people in your life won't do what you want just because you happen to be right.* They need to be persuaded. And if you're right, if it's in everyone's best interest that you get your way, it's not just your job to persuade them, it's your responsibility. Sometimes even your moral responsibility.

You're responsible as a parent to persuade your children to do what's right. It's your job to persuade your clients or prospects to make the best decision. You must persuade the person interviewing you to hire you if you're the right person for the job, and it's your responsibility to persuade your boss to approve your plans and budgets if they're the best for the company. You owe it to your friends, spouse, or parents to persuade them to make good decisions. If you're a professional salesperson, you owe it to your company and to your family to persuade people to buy what you're selling.

But you also have a responsibility to yourself to be persuasive, because there's little that can affect your life as profoundly as your ability to sell yourself, your ideas, and your services. It's the difference between having good ideas and having others put your good ideas into action; the difference between providing excellent service and having clients willing to pay you to provide the service; the difference between having the ability to lead and being given the opportunity to lead. If you're a professional salesperson, persuasion is the difference between being in line for a promotion and standing in the unemployment line.

Persuasion is the difference between having potential and achieving your potential. It's what connects being smart and working hard with making partner or vice-president. It's the link between being a caring parent and having your children embrace your values. It's an essential ingredient in turning a competent, trustworthy, hardworking Poet into a winner in everyday life.

Unfortunately, Poets sense a downside to persuasion. They know that the process of getting your way, of getting people to do what you want, can cause conflict and tension that can slowly destroy the relationship between persuader and persuadee. It's enough to make Poets think "It's not worth it." They identify persuasion with high-pressure, manipulative selling and cutthroat negotiation, and are often reluctant to persuade.

Get over it. Whether you're a parent, manager, CEO, teacher, job seeker, spouse, friend, or salesperson, persuasion is a natural and necessary element of life. If you hope to do what's right for yourself, your family, and the people in your everyday life, you *must* sell yourself, your ideas, and your services. But you must persuade gently, in a way that wins people's lasting respect, loyalty, and friendship, in a way that strengthens rather than hurts your personal relationships.

To persuade gently, you mustn't think in terms of winning or imposing your will. Instead, you must think of persuasion as effective communication. Specifically:

- Selling yourself means *communicating so effectively that people will accept that you are what you want them to believe you are.*
- Selling your ideas means *communicating so effectively that people accept your ideas as valid and valuable, and act on them.*
- Selling your services means *communicating so effectively that people use services you personally provide.*

Imagine the personal power of people who have mastered those skills. Imagine the difference it could make to you personally if you could consistently persuade people to do what you want them to do, and believe what you want them to believe about you, just through the power of effective communication. It's a power so valuable that most people would use a free wish to master it if they were to happen across the right magic lamp. It's right up there with fantasies like being able to read minds or see into the future.

Okay, snap out of it. Being able to persuade gently, to sell yourself and at the same time win people's respect and loyalty, doesn't require a magic lamp. When your ideas and proposals have merit and you persuade people through effective communication, you'll achieve your potential and strengthen your relationships. Life will be good.

That's why you need this book.

THE PLAN

There you are, facing someone you need to persuade, but someone whose goodwill you value. It could be a prospective client, but it could also be your boss, an interviewer, your spouse or your child. Maybe there's a lot at stake, maybe not. If you make the sale, and if it's done at no cost to your relationship, you'll achieve some part of your potential, you'll add another brick or two to whatever you're building with your life. If you're not persuasive, life goes on and nothing changes.

If you're like most people, you face this same situation several times a week, maybe even several times a day. You need a plan.

Three Steps to Yes is an ethical approach to persuading people. There are only three steps, because a hundred steps, or fifty steps, or even twenty-five steps are too many to remember, internalize, and use in the press of everyday life. Lots of steps means lots of complexity, and if it's complicated you can't make it a natural part of your life. If it's not a natural part of your life, your life won't change.

But the Three-Step Plan *can* change your life. It shows you how to deal with people so they'll do what you ask or believe what you want them to believe, even when competitors—the guy in the next office, your children's peers, rivals calling on your clients—try to undermine your efforts. And the plan shows you how to do it in a way that's not manipulative and that doesn't rely on selling and negotiating tricks.

The next part of this Introduction explains the difference between forced persuasion and gentle persuasion. Then the book treats each of the plan's three steps in three separate parts.

In Step 1, "Fulfill Personal Needs," you'll learn why people resist letting you get your way, and how to eliminate their resistance by focusing on their needs and anxieties instead of your own. We'll examine how to avoid consensus-destroying tension and conflict, and how to make getting your way a stress-free process.

In Step 2, "Be Credible," we'll identify the personal characteristics that determine credibility, as expressed through three core values that can entirely change your relationships with others and that, together, are almost a magic formula for becoming a naturally persuasive person.

In Step 3, "Communicate Persuasively," you'll learn how to tune in to how people listen and how they decide who and what to believe. We'll examine what you say and how you say it and learn to communicate so effectively that people will voluntarily let you get your way.

Twenty-one Gentle Persuasion Habits, spread throughout, are designed to help you put the Three-Step Plan into practice. These habits are no-nonsense, real-world advice on how to treat people you care about and how to communicate with them so you'll win their minds without losing their hearts.

The Three-Step Plan and the Gentle Persuasion Habits are not tricks for manipulating people or selling anything to anyone. They're principles that go to the heart of your personality and values, the way you think about and deal with people, and the way you communicate. The Three-Step Plan is simple, intuitive, and consistent with the value systems of all good people. If you live your life, treat people, and communicate according to the tenets of the plan, you'll be naturally persuasive and you'll get your way while improving the quality of your relationships. You'll win people's hearts as well as their minds.

Now that's a plan.

Gentle Persuasion

WHO OVERCOMES BY FORCE, HATH OVERCOME BUT
HALF HIS FOE.

—*John Milton*

I was an expert at persuasion long before I began the research for this book. My jobs required me to sell, negotiate, and persuade, and, at least early in my career, I went at it with a prideful vengeance. I knew all the classic approaches to selling, negotiation, persuasion, and influence, put them into practice, and taught others to do the same.

If you're out to destroy your personal relationships, the tactics I learned and perfected were ideal. Fortunately, age, experience, and survival instincts warned me it was possible to be too persuasive, that the cost of getting your way the wrong way wasn't worth the prize.

By the time I became a CEO, I was more concerned with long-term relationships than with just winning. I knew my old approaches were wrong, that they could wreak havoc on personal relationships, but I wasn't sure why, or what to do about it. So I abandoned all I had learned and, like most Poets, survived on instinct alone. Fortunately my instincts were good enough to carry me through, but I was always uneasy about the disparity between the conventional wisdom I'd learned so well and its wholesale rejection by the people it was used on.

Now I understand the problem with all the traditional approaches to persuasion—they use forced persuasion. They required me to personally apply an external force in an effort to get my way. I caused a negative reaction that opposed my persuasive efforts.

The concept of forced persuasion came to me while I was discussing Isaac Newton with my daughter, who was studying high-school physics. Newton's Third Law of Motion states that for every action there's an equal and opposite reaction. It applies to physical forces acting on physical objects, but I realized the idea applied to psychological forces acting on people as well. It explained to me why people resist being sold and persuaded, even when they're being persuaded to do something that's clearly in their best interest.

What I realized was that *people react not only to the ideas they're being asked to accept, but also to the persuasive force placed on them.* When you push them, their natural reaction is to resist, to push back. When people know you're trying to persuade them, the harder you push, the harder they resist.

As I thought more about it, I came to understand that I was relying on six forms of forced persuasion: authoritative power, punishments, rewards, traditional selling, relationship selling, and negotiation. If you're a manager, employee, parent, salesperson, professional, or any other Poet, it's a certainty you're doing the same thing. So it's important to know these approaches for what they are and to understand why, in the long run, they'll do you more harm than good.

FORCED PERSUASION

Authoritative power. "Clean up your room." "Have that report in by Monday morning." "Stop at red lights." People in authority can impose their will on others by virtue of their position.

But authoritative persuasion depends on both effective authority and forced compliance. When your children are young, you have effective authority over them. You can force them to go to bed by nine, go to school, make their beds, and stop fighting with their siblings. But if they're not acting of their own free will, when you're not looking, they misbehave.

The police have authority over drivers, but hidden cameras installed to photograph cars running traffic lights find that drivers regularly do it when they think they're not being watched. One camera, installed on a trial basis with enough film for what authorities thought would be thirty days, caught so many people running the red light it ran out of film in eight hours. In one community, hidden cameras installed at only 150 intersections caught 280,000 traffic violations in 1999 alone, resulting in fines of $19 million.

Authority decrees, it doesn't persuade; people who comply in response to authority are not persuaded.

For Poets, the real downside to authoritative persuasion is that when you force people to do something against their will, they usually start to dislike you. You lose their hearts.

We don't like the IRS, the state trooper who stops us for speeding, or the boss who forces us to work weekends. Children often come to dislike, or at least rebel against, parents who force their will on them. Enmity builds in spouses of partners who dictate decisions based on their assumed authority.

The trick to authoritative influence is not to eliminate it when it's for the general good, but to limit its use only to those times when you don't have a better option.

Punishment. Just because you have authority doesn't mean you can use it to get your way. You may be the boss, but when the economy is good and jobs are plentiful, employees can't be forced to do what they don't want to do. After a child reaches a certain age—and that age may be very young—parents find they can't simply tell her what to do and expect her to do it. A six-year-old will refuse to eat her carrots, and a teenager will decide he'd rather flip hamburgers and earn money for a car than study.

One way to persuade people to do what you want when you don't have effective authority is to threaten them with punishment: "No dessert if you don't eat your carrots." "There's a fifty-dollar fine and three points on your license for running a red light." "You can forget a good performance review if your project isn't done this month."

In the short term, there's no doubt this approach often works, in the sense that it helps you get your way. But it won't get you to yes, and it won't get you respect and loyalty. You won't win people's hearts. Nor is it self-sustaining; it will never get children to eat carrots on their own, employees to work extra hard, or drivers to stop at red lights when no one's looking.

The problem is that using punishment to persuade makes people feel like losers. If the person you're dealing with doesn't let you get your way, he loses by being punished. But if he lets you get your way, it could be an even greater loss, the loss people feel when they're forced to do something they don't want to do.

People who think they've lost never forget. They get even, finding ingenious ways to sabotage your efforts or otherwise make *you* lose. And when it happens, you won't even know there was a problem.

Rewards. A more positive approach to persuasion is to use rewards. The simple theme here is *If you do as I ask, I'll give you something in return:* "If you eat your carrots, you can have an extra dessert." "If you work this weekend, you can add the extra time you've worked to your vacation."

Using rewards instead of punishments is easier on your relationships, because you're not forcing people to lose. But from a practical standpoint it's a short-term fix. You can't give your six-year-old an extra dessert every night, and if everyone really does have to work weekends for an extended period, you're going to be in big trouble if everyone accumulates a year's vacation.

More important, you can't change people by relying on artificial inducements. Your child's not going to eat right when you're not around, and your employees won't go the extra mile without something in return. Stop providing the reward and you stop getting your way.

Traditional selling. Traditional selling is a collection of tactics, tricks, verbal manipulation, psychological strategies, and well-rehearsed question-and-answer scripts that salespeople have collected, refined, and passed down for decades. Their common thread is the salesperson pressuring a prospect to buy, sometimes subtly but more often not. Success is a closed sale. A positive long-term relationship is optional, a factor in the selling equation only if it leads to follow-on sales. Traditional selling is the epitome of forced persuasion.

It's safe to say that the salespeople who practice this approach are the salespeople buyers dislike, the salespeople who give selling its bad name. What's certain is that if you try to sell yourself, your ideas, or your services the same way traditionally trained salespeople sell insurance, used cars, or real estate, you're doomed.

If you use traditional selling tactics in a job interview, you're more likely to get the boot than an offer. If you use classic sales techniques on a good client, she will see you as manipulative, shallow, clueless—a bore. You might even be, egad, accused of selling.

Relationship selling. Buyers are fed up. Buyers, especially sophisticated buyers who purchase complex products for large organizations, are revolting against traditional selling tactics. They know all the classic selling tricks, have seen all the moves. These buyers have important responsibilities, wield real power, often earn big bucks, and have no tolerance for being manipulated.

Recognizing that the frontal assault is a losing strategy, modern sales trainers have developed branded selling methods that use guile, camouflage, and flanking maneuvers. Instead of relying on blatantly forceful persuasion and outright manipulation, these structured selling processes build on the concept of forming a relationship with the prospect or acting as a partner.

Although promoters position such selling approaches as buyer-friendly and relationship-sensitive, we shouldn't be fooled. For professional salespeople, closed sales pay the rent and failed ones don't, no matter how good a relationship the salesperson has with prospects who buy from the competition. It's not surprising, then, that it's a rare salesperson who, backed against the wall, puts forming long-term, personal relationships ahead of closing sales, making quotas, and supporting his family. Idealism and best intentions aside, when it comes to trading off long-term relationships against immediate sales, the relationships almost always take the fall.

But it can't work this way for Poets. Whether you're a professional selling to prospective clients, a manager persuading your employees, a parent persuading your child, or even a Poet professional salesperson who sincerely values your long-term relationships with customers, the people you're persuading are, and will remain, first and foremost an integral part of your everyday life. While it's essential for you to be persuasive, your priorities must be relationships first, persuasion second.

Negotiating. Negotiating has come a long way over the past fifty years. Initially identified with violent, hard-drinking, intransigent labor and management negotiators who made even the slickest used-car salesman seem like Mother Teresa, the art has gradually moved from win/stomp-into-the-ground approaches to (for modern, enlightened negotiators) win/win solutions.

Nevertheless, people still view negotiation as a process that takes place between adversaries sitting around a negotiating table, whether metaphorical or real, under conditions that are more or less a zero-sum game. It's a setting that makes relationship tensions almost inevitable.

For Poets, negotiating, even in its softest, gentlest form, is almost certainly inappropriate. There should never be the feeling, no matter how subtle, of a table with you on one side and your client, boss, spouse, employee, or prospective employer on the other.

And while negotiation requires compromise, compromise for Poets is often difficult, perhaps even irresponsible. There are no compromises when you're persuading your children not even to try drugs. If you're interviewing for a job, you either get it or you don't. If you settle for a 10-percent raise when you know you deserve 20 percent, and if your boss gives in to 10 percent even though he believes 5 percent is all the company can afford, the compromise may leave both you and your boss stewing and your relationship damaged.

THE FIRST LAW OF PERSUASION

Don't be misled by this criticism of forced persuasion; persuasive force is essential if you expect someone to do what you want. Something has to turn the potential energy of your facts into the kinetic energy of action. Persuasion without persuasive force is like starting your car but not putting it into gear. Without persuasive force, you'll wind up like the publicists I interviewed—presenting facts without persuading the person with whom you're talking.

The trick is to find the gentle persuasive force you need without evoking what we'll call the First Law of Persuasion, which is

Every persuasive force causes an opposite resisting force.

The corollary to this law is

People resist being persuaded.

The issue here is not that it's impossible to overcome persuasion-resisting force. In fact, the resisting force can be fairly easy to overcome if what you're proposing is very attractive or if the persuasive force you're applying is very strong. The issue is that even if you overcome the resistance to your persuasion efforts, you leave a residual feeling that hurts your long-term relationships. And this feeling can accumulate over time to do irreparable harm.

If you use a hard sell on employees, you'll have high turnover. If you force your child to study, you should be prepared for her to rebel when she goes away to college. If you impose your will on your spouse for years, you'll suddenly find yourself visiting your kids every other weekend.

To persuade without hurting your relationships, you need a beneficent persuasive force, a gentle force that doesn't cause a counteracting resistance. Fortunately, such a persuasive force exits, but *it comes from the person you're trying to persuade, not from you.* It requires that you persuade in a way that results in people deciding entirely on their own to let you get your way.

GENTLE PERSUASION

Gentle persuasion is *the art of communicating so effectively and compellingly that the people you're persuading voluntarily act in ways you intend.* The difference between forced persuasion and gentle persuasion is that with gentle persuasion, you're not applying a persuasive force, a force that's natural to resist. All you're doing is communicating. *The person you're persuading provides the persuasive force* and decides on his or her own whether to be persuaded. It's a big difference.

When the persuasive force comes from the person you're persuading and not from you, you avoid triggering the negative response of the First Law of Persuasion. But for this to happen, you must communicate so effectively and compellingly that your listener's personal needs motivate her to act without additional persuasive pressure from you.

As we saw with the three publicists, and as we'll see repeatedly throughout this book, communicating persuasively is not as easy as stating your case and expecting people to do what you want. Gentle persuasion requires persuasive communication, not just communication.

The Three-Step Plan deals at length with this idea of gentle persuasion, but some examples might be helpful here.

You're a lawyer talking to a prospective client who hasn't yet decided to sign on with you. If you've been trained in traditional selling, you might say, "I'm only able to take on one more client in March and one in April. In which month would you like to start?"

This is a traditional selling manipulation, called the double-option close, and only the most naïve buyer would be fooled. You're forcing your prospect to make one of two decisions favorable to you. The instinctive reaction of any buyer who recognized what you were doing would be to resist your manipulation, even if he started out predisposed to hire you.

If you're like most Poets, you shun this hard sell. Instead you describe your capabilities and hope your prospect is impressed enough to sign on. Unfortunately, because this approach lacks any persuasive force at all, it rarely works. "We work hard for our clients." (So what? I'm looking for results, not hard work.) "We provide the following services." (Great, so does everyone else.) "We have happy clients." (Everyone's got happy clients, and they've probably got some unhappy ones, too.)

This is exactly the approach used by the three publicists I interviewed. Although they avoided a negative reaction to forced persuasion, they weren't persuasive. There must be a persuasive force that moves your prospect to do what you want him or her to do.

But what if you took a third approach and said to your prospective client, who's facing criminal charges, "I'm a nationally recognized leader in criminal defense. I've successfully defended eighty-five clients in cases like yours, without a single conviction. I believe you have an excellent case and we can win. If you would like me to represent you, please let me know."

For reasons we'll discuss at length in the next three sections, this is persuasive communication. You need not provide any persuasive force, no hard sell, no double-option closes. You don't have to list all your credentials, where you went to school, or the law review articles you've published. If the client faces a threat to his freedom or economic security, his own needs will provide the persuasive force. Your prospect won't feel sold, pressured, manipulated, or forced to resist you. He'll voluntarily let you get your way. He'll be gently persuaded.

Let's take another example from everyday life. Your son won't study. If you threaten him with grounding if he doesn't get good grades, you're applying external persuasion he's sure to resist, even if he studies enough to meet your demands. It's resistance that can go on through his entire life, even long after he's independent of you.

What if, instead of using forced persuasion, you factually state that he won't get into Harvard without good grades? If he's too young to care about anything past tomorrow's Little League game, much less Harvard, you won't cause a negative reaction, but you won't be persuasive. This approach lacks persuasive force.

If your goal is to persuade your child to study and get good grades, and you want him to do it for the rest of his life and not just while you control him, you must find a personal need he has that studying fulfills, or, if no such need exists, you must help him develop one. If you can do this, your son will do what you want without your having to provide the persuasive force. This is gentle persuasion.

Unfortunately, creating a love of learning or a need to achieve is a lot harder and more time-consuming than telling your son that if he doesn't maintain a B average, he can't play baseball, or that if he gets all A's, you'll take him to Disneyland. But who said good parenting was easy? Fortunately the payoff is worth the effort. It's the only effective, ethical approach that will work and that won't result in resistance and conflict.

These examples illustrate the differences among forced persuasion, unpersuasiveness, and gentle persuasion. The key is that gentle persuasion happens not because of your authority or the selling or negotiation forces you apply, but because of your understanding of the people you're trying to persuade and how effectively you communicate with them.

We'll get to work on building this understanding in Step 1, and we'll talk about communicating effectively in Step 3.

Step 1

Fulfill
Personal
Needs

1

Why People Buy

Why do people smoke cigarettes or run five miles a day, go to church or to the golf course on Sunday mornings, hire you or someone else, obey their parents, or follow their peers? Why does your boss promote you or the guy in the next office, approve your plans or turn them down, do what you ask or find reasons not to? Why does your prospect buy from you or from your competitor? The answer is deceptively simple. We do what we do for one reason and one reason only: to fulfill our personal needs.

A need for food causes us to eat, a need for predictability to pull into McDonald's instead of Burt's House of Clams. We coerce our children to eat balanced meals because we need to protect and nurture them.

Like a vacuum, which diverts the speed and direction of the air around it until it's filled, personal needs are the invisible energy directing our behavior until they're satisfied. They determine what we do and how we do it.

There's a profound implication here: *People will do what you ask only if they believe they'll fulfill their own personal needs by doing so.* This is such an important idea that we'll spotlight it in the Second Law of Persuasion, which is

> *People will let you get your way if they believe doing so will fulfill their personal needs.*

Alternatively,

> *People buy if they believe buying will fulfill their personal needs.**

It's as simple as that, although, like $E = mc^2$, it's not as simple as it looks. There are interesting and subtle complications. First, the law doesn't say that people will *always* let you get your way if they believe doing so will fulfill their personal needs. Negative forces often conspire to keep people who intend or want to buy from buying, and we'll deal with these separately in chapter 7, titled "Why People Don't Buy."

Second, there's the word *believe.* It's not enough to fulfill people's personal needs; you must *persuade* them that you can do so. This important topic is covered in Steps 2 and 3. But before we worry about those issues, we need to understand personal needs.

Personal Needs

What exactly are these personal needs that cause people to do what you want? Fortunately for us, people all have similar personal needs. This doesn't mean that all people are alike. But

---

*As we talk about persuasion, we'll routinely use the words *buy* and *sell.* Sometimes they mean buying or selling in the classic sense of exchanging goods or services for money. But usually, saying someone "buys" is just shorthand for saying people agree to do what we want them to do, and "selling" simply means persuading.

what makes people unique is the difference in importance of the same basic needs.

We all have a need for acceptance and approval, but in some of us it's stronger than in others. Most of us care about wealth, but for some people it's their dominating motivator, while others care far more about their families or personal achievement.

If we begin by first understanding the basic needs we all share, we'll be better prepared to understand specific unique individuals. I've researched this subject of personal needs, and as you might expect, there's no generally accepted list. Abraham Maslow's well-known "need hierarchy" includes five needs, while other psychologists include twenty or more. One book on selling lists more than fifty, while Darwinian psychologists are happy with only one fundamental need: to procreate and send our genes off to future generations.

The problem of identifying basic human needs is not susceptible to indisputable scientific solution, and is thus subject to psychological, philosophical, religious, and semantic debates that, while interesting, will not bring you closer to getting your way. Fortunately we're not searching for scientific or philosophical truth. We just need a list that will work in practical, day-to-day situations, a list most Poets are willing to work with regardless of personal philosophical differences, and that helps us identify people's true motivations. It should not be so long that it's too cumbersome for Poets to use in the everyday situations they face, or so short as to ignore important motivations. I personally found the list below to be useful.

1. Physiological needs, e.g., food, air, water, sex
2. Risk reduction, security, and predictability—the need to prevent or protect against any negative change in the status quo
3. To have and rear children so they will prosper and have children of their own
4. Love and companionship

5. Enjoyment, fun, and intellectual satisfaction
6. To win
7. Consistency (i.e., the need for people to act and think consistently)
8. Recognition, status, prestige
9. Wealth
10. Acceptance and approval
11. To achieve or be the best
12. To show gratitude
13. To help others
14. To reduce guilt

I created this list based on my experience and study, and I've stress-tested it in hundreds of everyday-life persuasion encounters. It works and it's easy to use. If you have a different list, no problem. (For example, people who have studied human behavior include such needs as power, independence, uniqueness, and affiliation, and don't include some that I've included. Partly the difference is semantic, and partly it's due to the different intended uses for the lists.) But commit whatever list you use to memory so you can easily link what you're selling to the personal needs of the person you're selling to. And that leads us to Step 1.

The Three-Step Plan
STEP 1: Fulfill people's personal needs.

The Big Three

Fourteen needs may not seem like a lot as you sit in the comfort of your armchair reading this book. But when you're in the middle of a conversation with a real, live person you're trying to persuade, it helps to have an even shorter list in mind so you can focus on those few needs most relevant to the situation of the moment.

As it turns out, it's usually easy to spot which needs fit your specific circumstances. While everyone has these fourteen needs to some extent, different people in similar situations tend to be motivated by just a few similar and reasonably predictable needs. Moreover, the same people in different situations tend to be motivated by consistent personal needs.

A child motivated to win is generally motivated to win in nearly all situations over a long period. If your boss is risk-averse, he's likely to be so for as long as you know him in as many situations as you have to deal with him. If you're selling tax advice, all your clients are going to be motivated by the need for risk reduction, the need to win, or the need for wealth. To make your persuasive tasks easier, you should be able to look at the person and the situation and anticipate which needs might be most important before you jump into persuading.

In a later chapter we'll discuss how to identify the personal needs of the people you deal with, but no matter whom you're trying to persuade and no matter what the topic of discussion, there are three of the fourteen personal needs that are so universal that you should always be on the lookout for them. These three—the need to win; the need for risk reduction, security, and predictability; and the need for acceptance and approval—are such powerful forces in gentle persuasion, indeed, even in professional selling, that each warrants its own chapter.

2

The Need to Win

WINNING ISN'T EVERYTHING, BUT WANTING TO WIN IS.

—*Vince Lombardi*

It's a common misconception that, at least for the most part, people are rational. Easy mistake to make. After all, when you deal with people who are smart, educated, civilized, and well-mannered, you expect rational behavior. But what you often get is irrational thinking camouflaged as rational thought. If you don't understand this, you're doomed not to get your way when you should, or to hurt your relationships when you do get your way.

The problem arises because personal needs are deep-rooted and slow to change. As a result we often see what appears to be inappropriate or even irrational behavior from modern individuals responding to ancient drives. Nowhere is this irrationality more common than in the personal need to win.

Take the seemingly irrational need of many people to save a penny a gallon on gasoline, argue over the last fifty dollars on the price of a $50,000 car, insist that their child eat every carrot on her dinner plate, or fight climinating even a single person from their department's proposed budget. In the grand scheme of life—indeed, even in the light of the single transaction—the actual effect one way or the other is meaningless.

A tank of gas will cost fifteen cents less, the fifty dollars saved on the car is 2 percent of the utterly useless $2,500 "appearance group" option the buyer gladly paid for, the child will grow up healthy and happy even if she doesn't eat a single carrot for the rest of her life, and the company's earnings and the manager's career will be in no way affected if she goes through the year with one or two fewer people than she originally budgeted. Yet people go wild, seemingly irrationally wild, in a drive to win.

Rational or not, people have a deep-seated, often uncontrollable need to win, and you'll have an easier time getting your way in everyday life if you make them feel like winners. If you ignore people's need to win, or if you expect fair and rational behavior from everyone you deal with, you do so at your peril.

Unfortunately, you also have a deep-seated, often uncontrollable need to win, and it's often on its own campaign to make *you* feel like a winner and others feel like losers. That's the start of big trouble.

A Contest of Wills

If you, in even the smallest, seemingly insignificant way, set up a win-lose contest between you and the person you're trying to persuade, that person will resist letting you get your way.

Let's take the carrot incident, with which, as a parent, I am all too familiar. It begins when you tell your child to eat his vegetables, which you do because you want what's best for your child—good nutrition. This fulfills your compelling need to raise healthy children who, all parents hope, will provide grandchildren.

But your six-year-old child has no sense of mortality, feels invulnerable to life's vicissitudes, has little or no knowledge of nutrition, and is certainly not thinking about your grandchildren. Too bad for us parents, but to young children, eating carrots is not important.

Understand this fact: His eating carrots does not meet his personal needs. His eating carrots meets *your* personal needs. Eating ice cream, on the other hand—now we're talking *his* personal needs.

Let's say your child refuses to eat the carrots, perhaps not initially confronting the topic, but by spreading them around or hiding them in the mashed potatoes. Apparently the kid theory operating here is that you'll believe the reduced number of carrots per square inch is somehow equivalent to a reduced number of total carrots, or that you won't notice the half-inch lumps in the mashed potatoes. Whatever. Needless to say, you do notice, and before long, your good intentions and legitimate personal need to nurture your gene pool turn dinner into a contest of wills with a winner and a loser.

"Young man, I wasn't born yesterday." The trouble begins. You believe your six-year-old tried to pull a fast one, which is true. But it wasn't personal. That is, he wasn't trying to beat you at a game of "Hide the Carrots." He just didn't want to eat them. For him, that's a legitimate personal need.

But your hypersensitive need-to-win meter senses a personal challenge. The issue begins to shift from a need to nurture your child to a need to win. "No six-year-old is going to pull the wool over my eyes."

Now, your son has never read a book on selling or persuasion or taken a psychology course. But deep in the kid brain, his need-to-win sensor, which activated shortly after birth, picks up your need-to-win signals.

The game's afoot. Carrots, health, food likes and dislikes, and future grandchildren are no longer the issue. Far more is at stake—the need to win—and you and your child become engaged in a confrontation that neither will win, and that's destined to do collateral damage to your relationship. Not the least of this damage is an increased sensitivity on both sides to the other's need to win, a sensitivity that can grow to a point where, after a few years, neither of you can deal rationally with the other.

One thing this example illustrates is the subtle pervasiveness of persuasion in your life, and the extent to which it can unknowingly influence your personal relationships. The trouble begins when you get an idea in your mind and you, perhaps subconsciously, set out to influence someone. Your instincts tell you people will resist outright persuasion. So you're cool, mellow, laid back, sneak-attacking from the flanks. But few people are fooled. They usually know when to interpret your casual conversations, frank discussions, heart-to-heart talks, concerned questions, and spontaneous remarks as persuasion.

When you and your daughter pass a teenager with a ring in her nose and purple hair and you say, "What an idiot," your daughter knows what you're doing, even if you'd deny it to yourself. You're sending out a message that she'd better not even dream of piercing her body or dyeing her hair. She knows you're trying to persuade her, and she may react by resolving not to be persuaded.

If you tell your boss about a friend who landed a job just like yours in another company but who's earning 50 percent more than you're being paid, he probably interprets this as a persuasive message.

But what the carrot example also illustrates is how quickly and subtly persuasion motivated by productive personal needs can shift to persuasion motivated by a nonproductive need to win, and how damaging the shift can be to any attempt at persuasion, and to your ongoing relationships. If you really feel that what your children eat or the way they dress is a measure of your control over them, your kids will see food, clothes, nose rings, and purple hair as playing pieces in a contest of wills. Perversely, your daughter may dress in ways that not even she finds attractive, just to prevent you from winning.

Similarly, if you view getting a raise as a contest of wills between you and your boss, polish up the old résumé, because even the dumbest boss is going to fight you to the end, often even if he hurts himself and the company in the process.

Although you can't avoid persuasion, you *must* avoid shifting the substance of your persuasive efforts from productive needs to a nonproductive need to win. For there's one certainty in persuasion: *You lose all contests of wills.* Sometimes you lose them immediately, and sometimes only after a long time. But you always lose.

Creating Winners

To get your way in everyday life without hurting your relationships, make people feel like winners. It's not hard to do, if you just follow four simple rules:

• *Recognize when your own irrational need to win is influencing your judgment.* The carrot example above came from real life. I watched as a friend argued with his daughter about eating every last vegetable on her plate. She was negotiating to leave half of what remained, while he insisted that she eat every last carrot slice. His position was irrational in the light of whatever difference five carrot slices could make in the life of a six-year-old. But the harm to the relationship was manifest. He was out to win, not to look out for his daughter's best interests, and his daughter knew it.

So don't think about persuading as winning. If you're out to win, people will resist you at every turn. So, what can you do?

• *Give people more than they expect.* From every bill my friend Rob's accountant sends him, his accountant subtracts a discount he calls a "preferred client discount." The discount is not part of Rob's agreement with his accountant, and my friend has told me he always considered the bills fair even without the discount. But the discount makes Rob feel as though he's won something by having to pay for fewer services than he received.

I regularly let my son stay up past his bedtime on weekends without his having to ask me. I do this partially so he knows that when I lay down the law on important issues, it's not because I always have to win. Every time we do things his way without a fight or even a discussion, it helps him understand our horns aren't locked in battle. And if he forgets, I remind him that I've been very flexible with him in the past, but there are certain issues that, for his own good, aren't negotiable.

• *Don't disagree with people on unimportant issues.* Every time you argue unimportant points, you establish yourself as someone who needs to win—that you make the people you deal with feel like losers. Soon people will resist letting you get your way on both important and unimportant matters.

I watched as Steve, an in-house lawyer for a large company, insisted that all the language in a vendor's contract be changed to meet his demands. His legal arguments became nearly irrational and absurd, as he argued every point, no matter how insignificant. It was soon obvious to both the vendor and to Steve's client that Steve was out to win in what he saw as a contest of wills with the vendor's contract administrator.

Steve quickly lost the respect of both his client and the vendor, but the company's general counsel forced them to deal with him. Halfway though the talks, the client and the vendor quietly conspired to find ways to avoid Steve's influence. For example, when Steve wouldn't agree to the wording in the terms of one paragraph, Steve's client had the vendor slip it into a paragraph Steve had already reviewed. In the end, Steve turned out to be less persuasive than if he hadn't been assigned to the project at all.

• *Compromise early and often.* Agree to a lower base salary if you'll be given an opportunity for a higher bonus; be happy if your kid eats half his vegetables; agree to vacation in Florida in winter if your spouse will mountain bike with you in Moab this spring.

When he first read this, a colleague asked me how you avoid looking like a loser when you compromise. Wrong question. There's just too fine a line between working not to look like a loser and working to win. Make the other guy feel like a winner, and you can forget about winning or losing yourself.

A better question is how to avoid being taken advantage of by people who push to win everything they can. With such people, whether they're your children, your boss, your employees, or your customers, it's important to set unyielding, reasoned limits that you never compromise.

In business, I've always listened with an open mind to all requests managers and employees make for pay raises and bonuses. While I'm no pushover, within reason I try to accommodate all justifiable demands. When it comes to personal pay, I feel it's essential for people to feel like winners, perhaps even for them to believe they're earning more than they think they're really worth. If this means overpaying by 5 percent or so, it's a small price to pay to avoid a deadly business cancer— employees who feel they're being personally cheated, who feel the company they work for makes them losers.

Nevertheless, having employees constantly worrying about whether they could be earning more if they just asked hard enough and often enough is disruptive and counterproductive. So I set a few rules from which I never deviated. Perhaps the most important of these was that I never, ever allowed salary changes to be made except at two designated times during the year. Open-mindedness and flexibility notwithstanding, people came to accept that I'd talk about compensation two weeks each year, not fifty-two weeks a year.

My uncompromising position on this and certain other

compensation practices acted as a balance against my flexibility. People understood I was flexible out of fairness and not out of weakness, and didn't feel compelled to test my limits.

Gentle Persuasion Habit No. 1

Make people feel like winners. Never turn issues into win-lose contests. In the long run, you lose every contest of wills.

3

Security and Predictability

THE DESIRE FOR SAFETY STANDS AGAINST EVERY
GREAT AND NOBLE ENTERPRISE.

—*Tacitus*

The need to win is life's grease. It causes us to act, to take chances, to fight, to forge ahead despite whatever perils and negative consequences our actions might finally cause us. Both its greatest virtue and its greatest danger is that it focuses us on whatever positives we see in winning while blinding us to the costs if we fail. If the need to win had a slogan, it would be "Damn the torpedoes, full speed ahead!"

The need for security and predictability is life's glue. It causes us to stand pat, go slow, to embrace the tried and true, and to lock our minds and lives against the new and different. It focuses our attention on the dangers of changes to the status quo, and blinds us to the benefits. Its slogan might be "Whoa!"

Like the need to win, the need for security and predictability plays a starring role in gentle persuasion. It influences everyone to some extent, but on some people it has a near stranglehold. People with a high need for security and pre-dictability will see risks and danger where others don't, and will resist change with all the force of their being. For such people, change brings with it those most dreaded conditions, uncertainly and lack of control.

What makes the personal need for security and predictabil-ity difficult for Poets to deal with is that people in today's Western cultures don't accord this personal need much respect. Starting in grade school, people who worry about risk and resist new experiences are called wimps or chickens. It's the pioneers, adventurers, and entrepreneurs who get the respect and the movies made about them. Clint Eastwood stars as Dirty Harry the avenging cop, not as Steady Eddie the risk-averse accountant.

But Hollywood and social pressure notwithstanding, for many people low risk, security, and predictability are impor-tant. For some, these things are not just important, but all-important. But, to gain acceptance, many people deny this basic and dominant need they have. They may talk pioneer, but they act settler.

As a result, if what you're proposing in any way results in more risk or less security and predictability, you may never learn there's a problem until it's too late. People may deny that security and predictability are important, even to themselves. But when the time comes to actually make a decision, they will, often to your complete bewilderment, find an airtight, entirely rational-sounding justification that has nothing to do with risk, security, or predictability to choose the low risk, more secure or more predictable alternative.

I learned this the hard way. At one point in my career I had the good fortune to work for IBP, a Midwest-based Fortune 100 company revolutionizing the beef processing industry. The company was an exciting, high-growth manufacturing operation that, through innovation and no-nonsense manage-ment, was changing a moribund American industry.

To those of us who understood the industry, it was as exciting then as e-commerce was in 2000. But at the time, the company operated in what was perceived of as a rough-and-tumble environment replete with violent labor-management relations, negative press, and cutthroat competition.

Jim, a manager I was recruiting to join the company, was an intelligent, hardworking, Harvard Business School–educated executive who for years had been stuck at a dead-end job in a large Canadian company. Jim told me he hated his job, didn't respect the people he worked with, and was tired of living in a big city. Moreover, he was single, with nothing to prevent him from relocating.

I offered Jim a position with far more responsibility and visibility than his current job. The new job was a big promotion with almost unlimited opportunity, and it paid 50 percent more than he was earning, not even counting stock options. He'd be relocating to an area of the country with a higher quality of life and a much lower cost of living. In other words, joining us was a no-brainer decision.

Except that Jim turned us down. In explaining his decision, he talked about economic and business factors and opportunities at his current company, none of which made any sense at all. We knew he hadn't even told his current employer he was considering a change, so the issue wasn't that his present employer had made a great counteroffer. Instead of changing jobs, Jim stayed in his old company, in the same job, at the same pay grade, for five more years.

I stayed in touch with Jim, and ten years later, long after we had both moved on to other opportunities, I eventually learned why he had made a decision that at the time seemed almost irrational to me. As it turned out, Jim, like many other people, was risk-averse, with a high need for predictability. In my naïveté, when recruiting him I emphasized the excitement of the company and the industry, its growth, its unpredictability, and the seemingly endless supply of problems and unique business issues to deal with. In our discussions, Jim responded positively, professing to be excited by the opportunity and challenges. What I subsequently learned was that his reactions and his stated reasons for turning down the job at that time were all a smokescreen to hide his real need, which was for security and predictability.

Over time, I learned the power of the need for security and predictability in influencing people's behavior, and the extent to which people go to hide this need, even from themselves. To be safe, you should assume this need is a powerful motivator, even if the person you're persuading claims differently.

Your boss may profess to love your proposal to drop your company's traditional product line and move into higher-technology sectors, but in the final analysis he may decide, "The company has a responsibility to its customers and employees to stay the course. Besides, it's not in the shareholders' best interests to change the company's direction so dramatically. And security analysts wouldn't understand." And a whole lot of other folderol that has nothing to do with the real reason, which is that your boss just doesn't want to assume any personal risk. He doesn't want to risk making changes with unpredictable outcomes he may have difficulty dealing with, he doesn't want to make a decision that may not work out and that he's blamed for, and he may not want to face the prospect of presenting a proposal to his boss and risk getting turned down.

Or the corporate controller interviewing you for a job may think the year you spent living in a commune and your beard and earring are positive, refreshing signs of the independent thinking his company really needs. But he finally hires the plain vanilla, conventional, middle-of-his-class, clean-shaven CPA, because the controller isn't going to expose himself to a scintilla of criticism and career risk by hiring someone who may try to change things or whom his boss may not approve of.

You can even see this same unexpressed need for security and predictability in your family. Your spouse may spend eleven months planning a camping trip to Kashmir, but finally decides to vacation in Miami Beach because of cost and time considerations. Never are the risks of renegade bandits, heatstroke, or typhoid mentioned. Or he may talk incessantly about starting his own business and being his own boss, but he always has ten really great reasons to continue working for one big corporation after another.

As a Poet, you must be sensitive to people's personal needs for security, predictability and low risk, needs which are often evidenced more by past behavior than current talk. *Behavior* is the key here. Whenever you see a behavior pattern that indicates a high need for security and predictability, or you otherwise sense that these needs are important, deal with them head-on; they're the needs that will drive future decisions and behavior. Don't be misled, as I was by Jim, by the verbal smokescreens risk-averse people put up to hide their true needs.

There's one important rule for dealing with people you suspect have a high need for security and predictability, or any time your proposal can in any way be viewed as increasing personal risk: *No matter how exciting, new, original, or creative you personally believe your proposal is, always remember that these can be exactly the characteristics people translate to mean risk and unpredictability.* Emphasize your proposal's attributes that meet personal needs, not those characteristics that emphasize change and unpredictability.

It's one thing to tell your children that moving to California will result in the family living in a more temperate climate that allows them to play outside twelve months a year. It is another to say relocating means the excitement of moving to a new school and making new friends. While both may be true, being able to play outdoors year-round meets children's personal needs for fun, while making new friends emphasizes change and uncertainty. Which do you think would be more persuasive?

Gentle Persuasion Habit No. 2

Don't underestimate people's need for security, predictability, and low risk. Make your proposals as risk-free as possible.

4

The Need for Acceptance

PLEASE ACCEPT MY RESIGNATION. I DON'T WANT
TO BELONG TO ANY CLUB THAT WILL ACCEPT ME
AS A MEMBER.

—*Groucho Marx*

Fortunately for all of us, few people can get along in the world on their own. The boss, parent, or landlord may think he's king of all he surveys, but the king will soon find himself deposed without the support of family, friends, subjects, and peers.

If this weren't the case, if people could entirely fulfill their own personal needs, life would be ugly and harsh. People would be able to do whatever they wanted to meet their needs without regard for the personal needs and opinions of others.

This personal need for acceptance is often a key element that can work for or against Poets in gentle persuasion. Consider an experience I had with my son.

Zach is a baseball-playing, bicycle-riding, Rollerblading, cartoon-watching, 100-percent normal American boy, as are his friends. He's an intelligent, funny, articulate child whom we're working hard to bring up as a strong-willed, independent-minded person who thinks for himself and has the courage of his convictions. So I was surprised by what I learned when we discussed his buying new pants, an item of clothing he treats with the same care, attention, and respect that my cat gives to kitty litter.

I noticed that one pair of his Gap jeans still fit well, so I suggested that they didn't need to be replaced. His response was, *"Dad."* The word formed a complete sentence, followed with a slight sigh and a meaningful pause before proceeding with the conversation. This is the way we always begin conversations about subjects where my insight was gained in some parallel dad universe.

"Those jeans are too tight around the legs. My friends make fun of me and tell me I should get jeans that aren't so tight."

Now these were straight-legged jeans that were definitely not too tight. The cuffs easily fit over his boots. But who am I, a mere source of financing from planet Dad, to argue? So I asked him what he had in mind, hoping it wasn't a pair of those super-baggy jeans big enough to use as a drag chute for the space shuttle that I'd seen on some of the kids.

He had strong opinions about brands, and insisted on one in particular. When I took him to the store that sold that brand, he tried on about a dozen different pairs, searching for just the right coefficient of bagginess.

In the life of eleven-year-old boys in my son's school, pants bagginess was apparently an important factor in group acceptance. Not baggy enough and you're a "loser." Too baggy and you're a "poser."

His main criteria in selecting his pants was not how he thought they looked, but *what he thought his friends would think.* His buying decision was entirely driven by the need for acceptance by a group he was already a member of and who already accepted him 100 percent. This was just acceptance insurance.

The jeans he chose were acceptable to me, but if they weren't, it would have been impossible to persuade him to buy a different style without using my parental authority. Say

I was concerned what my own friends would think if I allowed my child to dress in a way they thought was not, somehow, "right." If I had forced him to buy what I was more comfortable with, it would have hurt our relationship. I would have overruled his very strong personal need for acceptance with a personal need of my own.

Remember this story when you deal with anyone, whether it's a boss, employee, client, family member, or friend. If the person you're persuading feels that he won't get the approval of the people whose acceptance he cares about, you must reevaluate your persuasion strategy.

Virtual Approval

Remember that approval doesn't mean formal approval and sign-off. My son was concerned about peer approval. Your spouse may be concerned about what his or her family thinks about the house you live in or the car you drive or the way you earn your living. Harley-Davidson, BMW, and Ducati motorcyclists need the approval of fellow Harley-Davidson, BMW, and Ducati owners they barely know. This virtual approval is no less powerful than the written approval your boss may need from the human resources department before he can give you the 20-percent raise you're asking for.

Here's a rule that can sometimes help you get your way: *Whenever possible, help the people you're persuading to win the approval they're looking for from others.* If you suspect your boss is hesitant to approve your hiring a specific individual because he's worried about what his boss will think about your candidate, deal with this head-on. Don't ask him to forget what others might think, or claim you'll take responsibility for the person's performance. This strategy doesn't address your boss's need to be accepted by his boss.

A better approach might be to suggest that his boss interview the candidate so she understands the candidate's value and will be supportive rather than judgmental. If that isn't possible, you can prepare succinct arguments that your boss can use to explain to his boss why the candidate would make a valuable addition to the team. While your boss may not need his boss's formal approval for you to hire your candidate, he needs her personal acceptance. If this acceptance is in jeopardy, you'll get rationalizations for why the candidate shouldn't be hired, even though, to you, the candidate seems perfect for the job.

Gentle Persuasion Habit No. 3

Remember that the people you're trying to persuade care about what others think. You won't get your way if what you're asking doesn't meet with the approval of others.

5

Situational Needs

Poets are fascinated by what they sell. The product, the service, the budget, the qualifications and résumé, the practice, the procedure, the proposal, the book, play, or article—this is what they think about, the thing they're most interested in. It may even be the center of their lives. So it's natural for them to think that what they're selling is what the people they talk to will be most interested in. These Poets are usually wrong.

As we've said, people are interested in fulfilling their personal needs. Unfortunately, the purpose of what we Poets sell is primarily to fulfill *situational needs*, which are the needs imposed on people by the particular life situation they happen to find themselves in. Only secondarily, and sometimes not at all, do our tangible products, services, ideas, and proposals fulfill personal needs. So we're enthusiastically selling something designed with an intrinsic purpose of fulfilling situational needs while the people we're selling to are choosing options based on how well they fulfill their personal needs. This causes a serious disconnect, a major breakdown in communications.

What we're selling, with all its benefits and wonders, all the great things it does and why it's better than other options at meeting the situational needs people say they have, is a "false north" that misdirects our interest, attention, and presentations. *Focusing on what we sell and the situational needs it fulfills is most often what stops us from getting our way in everyday life.*

To appreciate why so many Poets go so wrong, you need to understand the relationship between what you're selling and people's personal and situational needs. If you don't, you're too likely to inadvertently ignore our Second Law of Persuasion: *People will let you get your way only if they believe doing so will fulfill their personal needs.*

An Easy Mistake to Make

Consider a department head interviewing applicants for a job in her department. Of course there are certain minimum requirements an applicant must have: an engineering degree and a marketing background; ten years' experience in the industry; five years' P&L responsibility; and he or she must have managed a department of equivalent size or larger.

These are all situational needs—needs imposed on the interviewer by the particular situation his company finds itself in. Inevitably many candidates will meet these different situational needs, with none being clearly superior in all requirements. "The first candidate's got great industry experience, but is short on marketing background. Candidate number two has the marketing background but no P&L experience. Candidate number three has the right experience, but in the wrong industry. Candidate number four has everything, but seems like a jerk."

While the situational needs aren't irrelevant—the company's not going to hire a professional musician for a job requiring a professional engineer—it's not situational needs that drive the final decision. No manager will hire a qualified applicant if he's a threat to her job, or if he's someone she believes she'll hate working with, or if he negotiates salary so hard she feels as if she's in a war. Qualifications notwithstanding, when a candidate doesn't fulfill the interviewer's personal needs, he won't be hired.

Let's look at what this means from the standpoint of the applicant by listening in on a typical job interview:

"I earned my M.B.A. from Snooty U. and worked for eight years in investment banking at Rockem, Shockem & Dockem. Then I left to join Megabank, where I was part of the mergers and acquisitions group. I personally handled the $30 billion Global and Galactic merger."

He spends his valuable time with the interviewer trying to convince her that his education, talents, and experience match what she says the company wants. What could be more logical?

But if the interviewer will be a peer of the person hired, and will work alongside him on client projects, her personal needs may be for security and continued acceptance by her team. So while the candidate is enthusiastically talking about how his product (himself) will meet the company's situational needs, the interviewer makes her hiring recommendations based on whether she feels he's a threat to her job—and if not, whether the rest of the group will approve of her decision.

Buyers Are Liars

Let's look at an example where the commercial world and a Poet's everyday life come together. The Alberts visit Ellen, a real-estate agent, to find a home in the town they're moving to. Ellen, a good salesperson, begins by finding out the Alberts' needs: five bedrooms, a walk-in basement, a minimum of one acre; it must be in the best school district; under no circumstances should it have a swimming pool; and it is absolutely not to exceed a certain price.

These are the situational needs, the needs imposed on the buyers by their current situation—the number of people in their family, how they use their home, the children's ages, their financial circumstances. Most agents assume these are the needs that will drive their prospects' buying decisions. So they dutifully show them properties that meet the situational needs.

But after spending six months showing the Alberts every property that remotely meets their requirements, Ellen learns that her buyers bought, from a competing agent, for $100,000 over their not-to-exceed price, a home with four bedrooms, on a postage-stamp-sized lot, with a crawl space instead of a basement, in a mediocre school district, with a swimming pool. Ellen is shocked, and believes that their buying a house different from the one they swore they needed just reaffirms the old real-estate agent's adage, "Buyers are liars."

What happened was that the Alberts bought a home that met their personal needs, even if it didn't exactly meet their professed situational needs. The house they bought met Mr. Albert's personal needs for recognition, because it was in a more prestigious part of town and had a jaw-drop front entry that would impress visitors. Moreover, being unable to comfortably afford the house, the Alberts drove a hard bargain. Although the house cost far more than the family was originally prepared to pay, they got enough knocked off the asking price that it fulfilled their personal need to win.

The point is, the buyers made their final buying decision based on their personal needs, not on which home best met their situational needs. Ellen lost the sale because she listened superficially, hearing only the prosaic situational needs her buyers would admit to. She should have been on the lookout for the personal needs that drive home purchase decisions, which, for many people, are the needs for security, recognition, wealth (appreciation in value), and the need to win (by besting the seller). These are all far more powerful needs than the need for an extra bedroom so the in-laws can visit, even if all the buyers talk about is the extra bedroom.

Shifting Focus

Everyone you try to persuade is faced with both situational and personal needs, whether it's your boss who must approve or disapprove your budget, the graduating law student you're recruiting who is deciding which firm to work for, or your teenager who's deciding whether to get drunk with his high-school buddies or leave the party. While sometimes both situational and personal needs are best met by the same choice, *when they're not, personal needs prevail and people will find creative ways to rationalize their decisions.*

Unfortunately, Poets trying to persuade others always think people are looking for the alternative that best meets their situational needs. So they focus on proving that their proposal is better than competing alternatives at meeting situational needs.

But what people are actually doing is looking for the alternative that best meets their personal needs and that they can justify to themselves and others. So at some point, and it is not far into the persuasion process, *Poets must shift their focus away from situational needs and turn to addressing personal needs.* They must shift from thinking and talking about what they're selling to thinking and talking about the person they're selling to.

For the manager trying to get his departmental budget increased, this means a shift from why the increase is good for the department to why the increase will be good for the approving manager. Will it increase her chances for promotion or recognition, improve her job security, or make her richer? If all it will do is get her criticized by her boss, and if acceptance by her boss is an important personal need, you're playing a losing hand.

For the law firm recruiting new graduates, it means shifting the conversation from the wonders of the law firm and its partners to what the firm can do for the students who join.

If you want to keep your teenager from drinking, you must

stop talking and thinking about what you want as a parent, what you think is good for your child, what you think your child should want, or what you're going to do if your child doesn't do as you ask. In the end, all that really matters is your child's personal needs, whatever they may be and no matter what you think about them.

If the teenager has a high need for peer acceptance, he may stay at the party and get drunk, even though he knows he'll get sick, endanger his life when he drives home, and end up grounded. The personal need to be accepted by his peers is so strong that the child rationalizes ignoring his situational needs entirely.

On the other hand, if the teenager has a personal need to be accepted by his parents, or for the recognition as a student leader he'd lose by being expelled from school, his personal needs would be better served by finding some rationalization he can give his friends for not partying with them. "I'd like to stay, but my parents will take away my car." "Sorry, guys, I've got to work tomorrow." Somehow the child will find a way to avoid doing what doesn't meet his personal needs, *and you don't have to be there to help him do it.*

You must accept that, in the end, when your child is free to make his own decisions and you no longer exert total control over his behavior (which, of course, you never really did), he will act in ways that fulfill his personal needs. That being the case, if you hope to influence your teenager, only two strategies have any hope of working.

The first is to help your son understand how doing what you want him to do will fulfill his personal needs, entirely independent of what you may think of these needs. If you're a rabbinical scholar and really hate it that he's obsessed with becoming a professional wrestler, you can still use his need for success and recognition for his own good. Even though it may drive you nuts that he spends his time in the weight room instead of the library, when it comes to influencing his social behavior, it's still fair to impress upon your son that Hulk

Hogan didn't get to be a superstar with almost zero percent body fat through binge drinking.

The second strategy is to develop compelling personal needs in your child that are fulfilled by not drinking with his friends. This may be as simple as a need to earn *your* respect and acceptance by being his own person and standing his ground against negative peer influences, or a need to be accepted by a more positive social group, such as teammates or church members.

Every individual and family is different, and there's no common solution, except that you must help your child understand that certain behaviors fulfill *his or her* personal needs and others don't. What *your* needs are and what you want or think are largely irrelevant.

Gentle Persuasion Habit No. 4

Discipline yourself to think and talk more about people's personal needs and less about their situational needs.

6

The Other Guy
Talks First

Fine, you say. It makes sense that people do what they do to fulfill their personal needs. Like the high-school kid who knows smoking is bad for him but who smokes anyway, sometimes people will even ignore important situational needs (making the team) to meet personal needs (to look cool and be accepted by his peers).

But Poets typically ask at this point, "What if I don't know what people's personal needs are? Personal needs are . . . well, personal. How do I find out what's driving people's decisions if they won't admit what they want or need, maybe not even to themselves?"

The answer to this question is simple: Ask and listen. Unfortunately, those simple tasks prove to be hard for Poets in actual everyday life, almost unnatural. If you're doing the persuading, it's you who has something to say, a point to make, something to sell. Instinctively, it seems as if it's up to you to start the conversation, to make your points, to roll out a dog-and-pony show.

The people you're trying to persuade aren't much help. After years of persuasive assaults by salespeople, advertisers, employees, bosses, parents, children, teachers, the government, charities, public health groups, and others, people have come to expect the persuader to do the talking, to attack with information, logic, and self-serving reason. Steeled for the attack, they come to your conversation with their defenses ready, prepared to challenge, grill, and resist you. Even those who are open-minded have typically spent exactly zero time preparing for your conversation, so they're not prepared to cooperate, communicate, and talk, much less to do most of the talking.

You were lucky to get a thirty-minute appointment with your prospective client. She sure didn't spend an hour or two preparing for the meeting, thinking about what she wanted to get out of it, what her needs were, and what exactly she wanted to tell you. She's ready to listen to you do your thing; she's not ready to talk, to articulate her personal needs.

You've managed to get on your boss's calendar at the end of the day. When you walk into his office at 5:15, he's thinking about catching the 6:05 home to Greenwich, or whether his new car had its door dinged in the parking lot. He knows that the less he says, the faster he'll be on his way. He listens with his mind on the minute hand.

The interviewer you're about to meet had six previous interviews this morning and glanced at your résumé for maybe ten seconds before you walked in the door. You're lucky if she knows what position you're interviewing for. Anyway, she feels no need to prepare, because she knows you'll do all the talking.

Before you began talking to your son about college, he was thinking about an upcoming test, his girlfriend, or how to talk you out of twenty dollars for Saturday night. I can guarantee you he wasn't thinking about having a productive conversation about whatever it is that's on your boring adult mind. It's no wonder he sits there, as responsive as a paperweight, while you jabber on.

You go into these persuasion situations facing people who aren't prepared for a productive conversation and perhaps don't even want to have one. They're passive, waiting for you to talk. And you oblige.

Having a point to make or something to sell, and knowing your listener is in "receive" mode, your natural reaction is to transmit, to talk, not to ask and listen. If you're talking to a prospective client, you begin by describing your company and your services. If you're talking to your boss, you launch into the new programs you're planning with your proposed budget. If you're being interviewed for a new job, you drone on about your experience and education within two minutes of the handshake. If your goal is to persuade your teenager to attend your alma mater, you wax eloquent about what a good school it is and how its teachings helped you in your career.

Because the other guy's not talking, and you have something important to say, you burst out of the blocks as if there were a race to be run, a distance to be covered, a lot to be said, and you can't wait to say it.

Wrong mental picture. The persuasion process, especially its beginning, should be more Zen-like. What's needed is understanding and intuition, not a tour de force of reasons, logic, opinions, force of will, and brilliant repartee. Knowing what people are thinking is far more important than anything you have to say. Specifically, *you should know the personal needs of the people you're trying to persuade before you try to persuade them.*

Instead of telling people what's on your mind, encourage them first to tell you what's on their minds. Start by getting information flowing in the opposite direction—*from* the person you're trying to persuade *to* you. The only way to accomplish this is to follow the Third Law of Persuasion, the single most important rule of communicating, which is

The other guy always talks first.

Sometimes this is an easy assignment, but sometimes it's not. The challenge is that people are often not consciously aware of their personal needs, or may knowingly hide them from you or even from themselves. When this happens, they're reluctant to talk, or if they do, they talk around the real issues. Few prospective clients or bosses will admit that the overriding concern in their professional lives is to make decisions that will get them promoted, or that their compelling need is to get the approval of people whose opinions they shouldn't care about, but do. Interviewers won't tell you they just want to hire someone who's not going to make them look bad or take over their job. And your teenager may not have a clue what he wants out of college except to escape from seventeen years of your caring supervision and be "Thank God almighty, free at last."

So expect that the people you're trying to persuade may be distracted, circumspect, quiet, listening, receiving, and not transmitting. Expect them not to understand their true personal needs, or to be reluctant to describe them out loud. Don't take it personally—it's just human nature. If you ask the right questions, there's a good chance you'll get the answers you're looking for.

The Wrong Question

Unfortunately, it's generally not as simple as just coming out and asking, "Hey, level with me. What's really going to drive your decision here?" Ninety-nine out of a hundred people will respond with situational needs.

"Whaddya mean? I've already told you we're looking for a law firm that does intellectual property law." Or, "What's going to drive my decision? It's right in the job description. We want someone with an MBA, ten years' experience in high tech, five years' P&L responsibility, and a proven track record in marketing enterprise software." If you're talking with your spouse, maybe the answer will be, "Well, sweetie, you know I just want what's best for you." Or if you're talking to your teenager, "Huh?"

People aren't deliberately being obtuse or trying to mislead you. It's just that, more often than not, they don't give much thought to, or really understand, what's driving their decisions. Your prospective client or boss *thinks* he wants what's best for the company, but he *needs* what's best for his career and for his personal security. The interviewer *thinks* she wants a software marketing whiz, but she *needs* someone she feels comfortable working with. Your son *thinks* he wants a school with a journalism major, but he *needs* to win by being accepted at a more prestigious school than the one his sister's attending.

If even the people you're talking to are confused, what hope do you have? You're just a Poet, not a psychoanalyst. How do you even begin?

How to Begin

If it's important to you that you get your way, then you must begin by being deliberate. Before you ask your first question, before you speak your first word, before anything, you must switch mental gears from casual conversation to serious persuasion. You do this first by thinking about the person you're talking to in a slightly different fashion.

In professional selling, salespeople use the word "prospect" when they talk about the person they're trying to persuade. It expresses the idea that the person being sold to is a *prospective* customer or client. As such, a prospect is a valuable asset, and the term is one of respect.

Although it may be easy for Poets to think of a potential client or even a job interviewer as a prospect, it somehow seems strange to think of your boss, employee, friend, spouse, or child as a "prospect." "He's not a prospect, he's my pointy-headed boss." "She's not a prospect, she's the woman I love."

"He's not a prospect, he's my kid, and if he doesn't do what I tell him to, he's toast."

Ironically, the strangeness of thinking of people in your everyday life as prospects is the word's strength. Professional salespeople naturally identify the people they're selling to as prospects, as people requiring special attention. Salespeople dealing with prospects are deliberate, never casual or assuming. A salesperson would never say to a prospect, "Look, I know you want to buy a minivan because you've got six kids, but I sell Porsches, work hard, and need the commission, so buy a Porsche." Probability of a sale—zero. Probability of a meaningful long-term relationship—zero.

Poets also need to treat the people they persuade as special, but because these are the same people they deal with every day, there's a tendency to take them for granted. When that happens in a persuasion situation, Poets either don't get their way or they resort to forced persuasion and get their way at a cost to their personal relationships.

A husband, taking his prospect wife for granted, might say, "Look, I know you want a minivan because we've got six kids, but I work hard, I earn the money, and I've always wanted a Porsche, so that's what we're buying." Maybe a Porsche ends up in the garage, maybe not, but in either case the relationship suffers serious body damage.

Or the boss announces on a Friday afternoon, "I don't care how you do it, but this has to be out Monday morning." A parent shouts, "I'm sick and tired of telling you to clean up your room." An in-house attorney says to her client, "It's against the company's rules to sign any agreements without the legal department's approval." All these examples involve persuasion, and all fail to recognize that persuasion is not something to take for granted if you want to get your way and still preserve your relationship.

Because it's easy to hurt a relationship when persuasion is involved, you should recognize when the person you're talking to becomes someone you're persuading. So we'll use the word "Prospect" with a capital *P,* to identify the person you're persuading, whether that person is a prospective client, a boss, a subordinate, a peer, an interviewer, or a family member.

The Transition

You're cruising along, dealing with the people you always deal with, when suddenly some ordinary person in your everyday life—your boss, client, child, spouse, or friend—becomes your Prospect, and you become, whether you like it or not, a salesperson. If the issue is unimportant, for example, "Hey, get me a beer while you're up," don't give persuasion a second thought. But if the issue is important, you must click into persuasion mode. And as soon as this happens, it's time to stop talking. It's time to get the other person talking.

If you're a professional—say, a lawyer, accountant, or financial adviser—meeting with a prospective client for the first time, a poor transition from the casual banter that goes on whenever two people first meet to persuasion would be

> *Well, thanks for agreeing to meet with me. Let me begin by telling you about my company and how I might be able to help you.*

This doesn't work because you're doing the talking, you're assuming your prospect is interested in what you're talking about, and you're applying the persuasive force.

In contrast, a good transition would be

> *Before I talk about my services, it would help me if I better understood your objectives. Could you begin by telling me what you personally want to accomplish and why you're thinking of changing firms?*

If you're going into a job interview, your transition might be:

Before we start talking about me, I'd like to learn about you. How long have you been with the company, and what jobs have you held?

Note that these questions *ask about the person you're talking to, not about the company he or she works for.* Remember, although a company may wind up paying your fees or salary, you're being hired by individuals, not by a company. A company has no feelings, opinions, anxieties, or points of view; it doesn't care about winning or losing. So when people are telling you about their company's situational needs, they're not really telling you how they'll finally make their buying decision.

When selling to your child, trying to persuade her to accept your ideas, values, or just a specific suggestion, the transition from child to Prospect and from simple talk to persuasion might be

Barbara, do you mind it we talk about school for a while? I'd like to understand your curriculum and what the school expects from you in the eighth grade.

Whether your Prospect is a client, boss, employee, or child, you must craft a way to begin the conversation that is non-confrontational and nonjudgmental, and that gets the other person talking first. Confrontation and judgment set up the upcoming conversation as a win-lose situation, and you'll have the person you're trying to persuade setting up defenses before you take your second breath.

Even if every molecule in your body is crying out to tell your employee or child what you think of her performance, what you think she needs to do about it, and what you'll do if she doesn't, this approach won't be persuasive.

Signaling

Sometimes getting the other guy to talk first is tougher than it sounds. People aren't always forthcoming or they wander off into irrelevant discussions. They're not purposely giving you a hard time. They just don't know what kind of answer you expect or what answers are safe.

If you ask a prospective client at your first meeting to tell you her problems and how you can help her, don't expect a useful answer. Most of her problems are none of your business. And she may have no idea how you can help her, short of your leaving as soon as possible so she can get back to work.

If you ask your teenager to tell you about school, you can pretty much guess where things are headed—eyeballs north and the conversation south.

Questions don't get the other guy to talk first if they're too open-ended. You need to *signal* the kind of answer you're looking for—and maybe even the kind of answer that's safe to give.

If you're a financial adviser asking your prospective client about his financial plans, you can't be sure you'll get a useful response. Maybe he never thought through financial goals and will tell you what he thinks you want to hear, or he'll tell you what will make him look good. Or maybe you'll get back an embarrassed stare. But you might instead begin with:

> *One of my specialties is helping parents finance their children's college educations without having to tap into their retirement savings, mortgage their home, or force large loans on the kids. What issues do you foresee in financing your kids' college educations?*

You've spent maybe fifteen seconds talking about yourself, but only as a signal so your Prospect knows how to answer your questions. If he's concerned about financing college costs, you're now ready to spend the next thirty minutes listening to and talking about your Prospect. If his concerns lie elsewhere, you'll know that too and can take the conversation in a new area, say, preparing for retirement.

This is far different from spending the first thirty minutes talking about yourself and your services and getting around to your Prospect only after you've impressed him with the wonders of whatever it is you're selling. And it's far more effective than asking very broad and open-ended questions that leave your Prospect wondering what you're getting at.

You're worried because your daughter's not performing up to her potential at school and you suspect the negative influence of one of her friends. If you drone on about your opinion of her friend, the importance of not giving in to negative influences, or any other typical parent lectures, she's not going to listen to you, much less talk about her problems. And if you ask her to tell you how things are going at school, or to talk about her friends, or about what's worrying her, you're probably in for a very short conversation. So what's the plan?

Signal what's appropriate and safe to talk about. What works best depends on the history of your relationship, but one possibility is telling her something that happened to you when you were a child.

> *I never told you this, but when I was in high school, I went through a bad time. I was a pretty good student, but then I started to hang out with kids who thought it wasn't cool for girls to be smart. It took me nearly a year to figure out the problem was that a couple of them just weren't smart and the rest were lazy, but my freshman year was a disaster. I spent my entire sophomore year making up for lost time. I know you really look up to Ann, but I wonder if you're going through a little bit of the same thing I went through.*

What you've said is nonthreatening and targets the conversation so that she knows what to talk about. By admitting to your own past problems, you've signaled that she can safely talk about a similar problem she may have.

The point is that to get the other guy to talk first, *you* sometimes have to talk first—but only a little. You send a signal that opens communication channels, makes the other guy comfortable, and lets him know how to answer your questions.

A Special Bonus

An interesting benefit of getting the other guy to talk first is that you might find people reciprocating, beginning to take the needs of others—sometimes even you—into account. My friend Dominic had always had a difficult time talking with his son, Anthony. Although there were no specific problems, their ability to communicate and Dominic's influence over his son continued to lessen until, at fourteen, Dominic was barely a factor in Anthony's life. This became particularly troubling as Anthony's school performance deteriorated.

After reading an early draft of this book, Dominic stopped talking to his son and began asking questions in an effort to understand his needs. He told me the transformation was remarkable. For the first time in years, they had real conversations together and decided to make changes in Anthony's high-school plans.

But, even more important, Dominic began to notice a distinct change in the way Anthony dealt with him. While his son didn't have the persuasion tools to be sensitive to and search out his father's needs, Anthony became, almost overnight, much more patient with his father.

For example, Anthony would rarely ask for help with homework, but when he did, he'd act as if his father were ignorant if he didn't remember arcane facts or was unable immediately to solve tricky math or physics problems. Dominic tells me his son is now far more understanding about the fact that his father received his primary education in Italy and isn't familiar with many of the subjects taught in American schools.

They made a deal that Dominic tells me wouldn't have been possible before he changed the way he dealt with his son: If Anthony needs help with a subject his father is not likely to know well, he gives his father the supporting material to read. *Then* they work together to answer Anthony's questions. A downward spiral has turned into a positive relationship.

Bat Listening

Now comes the hard part. When you've got the other person talking, *you've got to listen!* Not just listen, but really, really listen. Listen so you don't just *hear* what the other person is saying, but so you *understand* what the other person is saying, maybe understand even better than the person who's saying it. To help, use a technique I call "bat listening."

Human beings see and hear passively. That is, they can just sit back and passively receive light and sound waves without actively participating in a conversation. That's why you can never be truly sure you're getting through to the person you're talking to, but it's also the reason you may not be truly listening to the person talking to you.

Bats use an entirely different mechanism, echolocation, which requires their active involvement and demands that they continuously process what they "hear." Like sonar on a submarine, bats send out signals, typically ultrasound, that bounce off their targets—insects, trees, the windshields of eighteen-wheelers—and get reflected back for immediate processing by their bat brains.

Given this need to listen to and process every incoming signal, bats are definitely not big-picture creatures. Unlike us, they can't just sit back and passively listen and decide what to do after they've heard the whole story. They can't ignore intermediate information they receive and tune in and out of their conversations with the outside world, confident they'll pick up the gist of what's being communicated. They navigate, deciding which direction to fly and what to do next, based on what they learn as they go along. If they stop paying attention, they're dead bats.

The human brain is far larger than an entire bat. For better or worse, we can do such things as conceptualize, summarize, judge, store for later processing, or ignore the vast quantities of data we hear and see. In terms of raw IQ, we've got it all over bats. But when it comes to listening, these abilities, which give us the option of tuning in or turning off what's being said, might actually put us at a disadvantage. When it's important that you listen, particularly if you're flying into the unknown, try to listen like a bat.

Specifically, send out a signal, wait for a response, listen to the response, then think about it before you decide what you're going to say. Only after you've done all that should you send out another signal. There are three important concepts here. The most important is that *you're talking to listen and understand, as opposed to talking to be heard.* The second is that you're listening carefully to every response that comes back from the signals you send out. Finally, you're navigating, adjusting what you say and do, according to what you hear as you go along.

To make this work, at a minimum, you have to stop talking so you can listen and think about what the other person is saying. For example, after asking your transition question, stop talking. Don't just stop talking, don't even think about talking. No matter how long it takes your Prospect to answer, think about only one thing: listening—because listening is the only way you can learn about the personal needs of the individual you're trying to persuade.

Don't worry about not getting back responses to the signals you send out. People like being asked about themselves, and they'll spend anywhere from five minutes to an hour—or more—answering thoughtful questions *from someone who is sincerely interested in them,* someone who's listening and not interrupting, someone's who's not just waiting for an opening so he can say what's on his mind. How long people spend talking to you, and how complete an answer they give you, depends largely on your interest, which you express best by paying close attention and by asking intelligent follow-on questions.

With a little luck and a lot of attentiveness, you may figure out your Prospect's personal needs just from her answer to your transition question. If you do, you're ready to link your proposal to her personal needs. But if your Prospect's story doesn't help you understand her personal needs, *you're not ready to persuade her.*

You may be raring to present all your good stuff, but you're not going to have a persuasive conversation. So don't start broadcasting. Ask more questions, questions that will help your Prospect describe her personal needs. You've got to send out more bat signals.

As you listen, you'll find that some people can easily describe their personal needs, while others have a great deal of trouble with it. Your boss may know exactly what he personally wants from your efforts, but your child may be utterly confused about what he wants out of school, sports, his family relationships, or life generally. The questions you ask next are meant to help people understand and describe their personal needs by helping them visualize and talk about the present, past, or future.

Asking Directly

The simplest and most direct approach to learning your Prospect's needs is to come right out and ask. If you're a professional selling to a potential client, you might phrase your question this way:

> *Looking at this decision to pick a law firm from your standpoint, and not from the standpoint of your company, what is it you're looking for?*

If you're talking to an interviewer, your question might be as follows:

As someone who'll have to work with whoever's hired, what are you personally looking for in the right candidate?

If you're talking to your elderly mother about selling her large, old, and unaffordable house and moving to a nearby retirement community, you might ask:

Mom, I know you've lived in this old house a long time, and it has a lot of memories. But things have changed. What is it you want from wherever you live for the next ten years?

With most people, this direct approach encourages them to think through and articulate their personal needs. Frequently they'll first answer by listing situational needs, for example, "I want the most cost-effective solution for the company." When this happens, try again. "Yes, I understand those are your company's needs. But what are you personally looking for? What's most important to you personally?"

If your mother responds to your question by answering, "Oh, I want a house big enough for all the kids to come visit during the holidays," this is a situational need. Her personal need is for love and companionship and connection with her family. Or it might be the security and predictability of being in a place she's familiar with, or the companionship of her longtime neighbors. If you focus on her personal needs and not her situational needs, it's far more likely you'll persuade her to make a change that's best for her.

If you're dealing with children, say, having that talk about your daughter's performance at school, this direct approach won't work unless she happens to be especially mature and directed. One child may know exactly what she wants out of school while another is feeling his way, going to school each day only because that's what kids do.

A child who hasn't yet formed ideas about his enduring personal needs will not be able to answer this open question. You need to move to one of the other approaches.

The direct approach is remarkably helpful with perhaps 50 percent of the people you'll meet. You can almost see a light go on when they understand what you're asking. "Oh, I see what you mean. I've got to be sure that the system we buy works so I'm not left trying to explain my failure to the board."

But for the other half of the people you deal with, this direct approach won't be enough, because your Prospects simply don't know what they want personally from a decision, or are reluctant to state it. When this happens, there are other questions for getting to Prospects' personal needs more indirectly.

Looking Forward

Here's a typical forward-looking question:

> *Let's project into the future. What do you visualize as the ideal outcome? How would things work if you could write the script and everything went as you'd like it to go?**

This question helps Prospects formulate and articulate their objectives and needs. If their answer is centered around situational needs, such as their company's needs, you can ask: "I understand how this would work for the company, but how do you see this benefiting you personally if everything went the way you'd like?"

Looking Back

If looking forward doesn't help you understand your Prospect's personal needs, the next question looks back. It asks people about the shortcomings of their current or past circumstances.

---

*I've found the exact wording of these three sentences to be particularly effective for helping people understand what they want to accomplish.

This approach is sometimes more successful, because it's generally easier for people to talk about what they don't like about a situation that actually exists than to visualize and describe a future solution that doesn't yet exist. The question is simply this:

> *It would help me understand what the best outcome in the future would be if you'd describe what you don't like about the current (or past) situation. From a personal standpoint, what changes would you like to see?*

This is particularly helpful to people who are unhappy and want a change, but aren't sure why. By articulating what they don't like about their present situation, they (and you) get a better understanding of their unmet needs and of what might work going forward.

Let's Compare

The comparison question asks Prospects to describe what they like and don't like about options they're considering. The question might be phrased this way:

> *I'm sure you're looking at other options. What do you personally like about the best options you've seen so far?*

You're asking your Prospect to compare concrete proposals she's already heard; this is often an easier way for people to express their needs than having to visualize and describe the future.

What Do You Think of This?

There are a few times—very few—when Prospects are uncommunicative and none of these approaches works. For example, it's unlikely anyone will ever say, "I have a compelling personal need not to be fired before I retire in three years. I don't care what's in it for the company, I'm not making any decision that has any personal risk for me whatsoever." Similarly, children are often uncommunicative because they're too young to know their own needs or simply have not yet learned to express themselves.

So, despite all your best efforts, you may have to begin talking without a good understanding of your Prospect's personal needs. With what we'll call the "incremental feedback" approach, you begin talking about what you're selling, but emphasize the different personal needs your proposal fulfills. After you discuss each need, you stop talking and ask for feedback from your Prospect.

If you want to be hired as a consultant—say, for a mergers and acquisition assignment—you might begin with a description of one particular past assignment, and ask questions like these:

> *The assignment we did with Intergalactic Systems illustrates how we work to increase the price per share for you and other shareholders. Is this your primary concern, or is it more an issue of finding the right strategic partner that will preserve the management team?*

Notice that this question focuses on personal needs (wealth and security), and not on what you think are their situational needs.

If you're talking with your teenager about school, the question might be, "What is it you like or don't like about the subjects you're taking at school?"

Of course, the answer will be something like "I dunno," or "They're all just boring," or "All the stuff we're learning is useless in real life." Great, at least you're got a conversation started. Granted, it may be the barest rudiments of human communication, but at least it's a place to begin. You can now plant some positive ideas, but don't lecture. Continue to ask questions and encourage your child to talk about what most interests him—himself.

"I'm sorry your classes seem that way. You always did well in science and seemed to like it. How's that going this year?"

Your goal is to help him discover what his personal needs are, and how his schoolwork relates to them. It's an objective you won't achieve in a single conversation, and maybe not even in dozens of conversations over several years. But until he and you understand his personal needs and how school helps him achieve them, you won't be persuasive in changing his behavior.

Working Together

None of this questioning is designed to manipulate people into saying what you want them to say. Your goal is to engage in a search with your Prospect to find the compelling reasons why he or she should let you get your way.

It's entirely possible that the initial result of this search will be that you discover there are no such compelling reasons. There may be no personal needs your boss can fulfill by increasing your department's budget by 50 percent, even though what you're proposing is good for the company. There may be no compelling personal need your prospective client can fulfill by dropping his current supplier and signing on with you, even though you have a better product at a lower price. There may be no compelling need your daughter fulfills by attending an all-women's college, even if you both know that's where she'll get the best education.

When this happens, your search shifts to finding ways for you to change what you're asking for, so that your Prospect's personal needs, whatever they are, are fulfilled. Perhaps you change your budget request from a 50-percent increase to a 52-percent increase to cover the additional cost of bringing in an outside expert to ensure that the new high-tech project you're proposing doesn't fail and leave your boss with a serious career problem. Or you provide your prospective client with prestige and recognition by arranging for him to make the keynote speech at an important industry meeting if he signs up with your firm. Or you agree that your daughter can spend her summers in Europe and her junior year at the Sorbonne so she can supplement the social life she's afraid she'll miss at a women's school.

Notice we're not talking about negotiating here. You're on a search to find a way to fulfill your Prospect's personal needs, not for a compromise she may feel forced to accept but not be happy with. What you're doing is leading a search to bring whatever you're proposing into line with whatever your Prospect's personal needs are.

If you don't like your Prospect's personal needs, that's tough. Unless those needs are immoral or unethical or you're dealing with children too young to have formed enduring, productive needs, it's not your role to judge people's personal needs or to try to change them. If what you're selling can't fulfill your Prospect's personal needs, you may be selling the wrong thing to the wrong person, and you should reconsider.

In any case, it's essential that you know your Prospect's personal needs *before* you launch into what you want to say. It won't help to propose bringing in an outside expert if your boss is worried that your project's success might lead to you taking over his job. It makes no sense to propose summers in Europe if your daughter's concern is being away from her boyfriend.

The only way you're going to figure out your Prospect's personal needs is if your Prospect talks to you. Which leaves you less time to talk about what you're selling. Don't panic. People like talking about themselves as much as you like talking about yourself. *I have never had a conversation or meeting cut short because a Prospect spent too much time talking about himself.*

Think how much more effective and efficient your presentation will be when it's targeted to, and only to, the concerns and needs of the person on the receiving end. What could make more sense than to talk about what your listeners are interested in, and to continually relate what you're saying to the needs they've just expressed? All that's required is the courtesy of letting the other guy talk first, helping him think about and articulate his needs through well-prepared questions, and, perhaps hardest of all, actually listening and adjusting what you say.

Gentle Persuasion Habit No. 5

Let the other guy talk first. Always begin by asking questions and listening—really listening. Before you try to persuade people, you must understand their personal needs and how what you're proposing might fulfill those needs.

7

Why People Don't Buy

JUST WHAT EXACTLY IS IT YOU DON'T UNDERSTAND
ABOUT "NO"?

If only selling and persuasion were as simple as demonstrating you can fulfill people's personal needs. But, as we've warned, sometimes people don't buy, even when they think their personal needs will be met.

The problem is that when you ask Prospects to buy, you cause emotional stress by putting them between the desire to fulfill their personal needs and five buying anxieties. Present to some degree in all decisions, these are

1. Reluctance to give up options
2. Fear of making a mistake
3. Social pressures
4. Fear of losing
5. Perceived cost

You may be able to think of other reasons that people don't buy even when they think their personal needs will be met, but in my experience, all buying anxieties boil down to these simple five. For example, when people don't buy because they're afraid they might be able to get a better deal elsewhere, they're really afraid of losing. If they hesitate because they're concerned things might not work out as you say, they're afraid of making a mistake. If you're the first person the interviewer has met and she won't make you an offer because she wants to meet other candidates, she's reluctant to give up options. If your daughter refuses to lose the green hair and nose ring even though you both know she looks ridiculous, her anxiety is about social pressure from her peers.

As with personal needs, our objective is to simplify things, and reducing all buying anxieties to five is pretty simple. After all, Poets have enough to think about. But we need to understand these five if we hope to get our way.

Loss of Options

People value the freedom to choose. Unfortunately, if agreeing with you forces someone to give up other options, this works against you. Research shows that *whenever people think their freedom to choose is limited or threatened, they want what they can't have more than they did before they lost the option to have it.*

Consider my friend Steve, who was thinking about buying a second motorcycle. He didn't need a second motorcycle (trust me, no one "needs" two motorcycles), and he had no free garage space at home to park it. Everything was more or less under control, even after he learned about a good deal on a three-year-old bike with less than one hundred miles on it. It was the make and model he wanted, but he still waffled. He wasn't even willing to drive down to the dealer to see the bike.

Then he learned that someone else was excited about buying the motorcycle and had gone home to discuss it with his wife before making the final decision. Believing he was about to lose the option to buy the motorcycle, Steve immediately bought it over the phone, sight unseen.

Marriage is a classic example of the effects of loss of options. The closer the happy couple comes to the wedding date, the more likely it becomes that either the bride or the groom or both of them are worrying about the impending loss of the single lifestyle, and the more they start to question their decision.

I'm convinced that the only reason many weddings take place is that the matchbooks have been printed, the hall rented, and the invitations mailed. The loss-of-options anxiety is shouting in the brain of bride or groom to call the whole thing off before it's too late, but the emotional and financial costs of canceling the wedding—which seem so much more onerous than actually going ahead—keep things on track.

But sometimes not even cancellation cost or inertia is enough. One of my wife's longtime friends was due to be married in a big Manhattan wedding. The morning of the wedding, the guests learned at the church door that the couple had changed their minds. Talk about buying anxieties increasing as the final decision approaches!

A funny example happened to my wife, Deborah, when it came time to trade her two-seater sports car in for a full-sized vehicle. As we waited for the new car to arrive at the dealer, she lamented the loss of her sports car. Then, when the car arrived, it looked as if the dealer was going to try to change the agreement we'd made, and I refused to go along. When I told Deborah, her immediate response was, "Damn, now we're going to be stuck with my old car." This was an instinctive reaction to losing the option of buying the new car. It was a 180-degree shift from the reaction she'd had when she thought she was about to lose her old car.

But within a few hours the dealer came around and decided to honor our original agreement. When I told Deborah, she again wasn't sure she really wanted to trade her old car. Another 180-degree shift caused by a perceived loss of options.

What made this interesting is that Deborah had proofread the part of this book on loss of options many times. Even though she knew what was happening, she couldn't help feeling the loss-of-options buying anxiety, first when she thought we were buying a new car, then when she thought we weren't, and then again when she thought we were.

So, if you're asking someone to make a choice, it's a problem. As people come closer to doing what you ask instead of something else, the attractiveness of the lost options increases and makes it hard for them to make a decision. It's a perverse aspect of human nature that works against getting your way in everyday life.

Fear of Making a Mistake

If life were perfect and buyers never made mistakes or had bad buying experiences, there wouldn't be a fear of buying. Buyers could decide which alternative was most likely to meet their needs, and could easily make decisions.

But life isn't perfect, not even close. Your new suit fit badly, the guy in the next seat paid less for his flight, you really can't hit a golf ball fifty yards farther with your new $600 Strontium 90 driver, your PC was obsolete the day after you threw out the cartons, your lawyer lost your case. Instead of fulfilling your personal needs, buying turned out to be a disappointment or a loss—a punishment. This happens often enough in everyday life that, many times, people don't buy simply because they're afraid they'll make a mistake.

This fear of buying can be caused by a lack of trust in the person doing the persuading, past bad experiences with similar decisions, uncertainty about whether buying will fulfill a real personal need, or other factors. But whatever the reason, as your Prospect gets closer to deciding, he also gets closer to the chance of making a mistake. If he's seriously worried that agreeing with you might be the wrong thing to do, he'll back away just when it seems that a decision is imminent. You're left wondering why it's so difficult to get your Prospect to decide, even when the right decision seems so obvious.

Social Pressures

Although people buy to fulfill their personal needs, they always make their buying decisions with an eye on others' opinions and reactions. So, while you must fulfill your Prospect's personal needs, don't forget that she must still justify her decision to others.

If you want your boss to approve your budget increase, you must not only justify it to her, but you must also help her justify it to her boss. If you want your child home by 10:00 P.M. on weeknights and all his friends stay out past midnight, give him a way to justify the curfew to his friends.

A favorite tactic for both children and parents is to blame everything on the parents. When it came to dating, my friend's daughters told their friends, "I'd like to date, but *my parents won't let me* until I'm sixteen." With this simple phrase, "my parents won't let me," the girls justified their actions to their friends. In fact, the girls were relieved not to have to date before they reached sixteen. My wife and I like this approach so much we tell our children they can blame us and say "my parents won't let me" for their refusal to do anything they know is wrong or they just don't want to do.

Again, this buying anxiety builds as your Prospect comes closer to making a decision and has to explain it to others. If your Prospects can't come up with reasonable rationalizations, they back away from buying even though they want to buy. And again, you're left wondering why your Prospect doesn't make a decision that seems so logical to you.

So you must not only show Prospects that their personal needs will be fulfilled, but you must also give them the buying rationalizations they need to get others to approve of their decisions.

Fear of Losing

The fear of losing is the flip side of the need to win. Because evolution doesn't favor losers, the fear of losing is so programmed into our DNA that we do all sorts of things, both rational and irrational, to avoid losing. We don't let people cut into line, we compete in meaningless games and sports as if our lives were at stake, *and we will never buy from or agree with someone who makes us feel as if he's about to win and we're about to lose.*

People react to win-lose situations the way Superman reacts to Kryptonite. They can sense the slightest trace of it anywhere. If they believe they can't win, they immediately run. If they sense they can win, they stop at nothing until they do. Either way, you lose. The fear of losing is so strong, it can even stop people from making decisions that overwhelmingly meet other personal needs. If your Prospect feels he'll lose by doing what you ask, getting your way will be a continual struggle, a struggle *you're* sure to lose.

I personally experienced the power of this fear-of-losing anxiety. On a business trip to meet with a client, I flew into the Atlanta airport. Having to get to the client's office outside of town, I went to the only taxi in line and asked the fare. The driver quoted a flat amount that was less than half of what it would cost me to rent a car, but high enough to make me think he might have been overcharging me by a few dollars. I refused to get in his cab until I checked the fare with other taxis.

As I walked around on a hot, humid Atlanta afternoon looking for another cab and lugging my suitcase and briefcase, I realized I was being stupid. The cost of the ride was going to be charged to my client, who would gladly have paid the relatively small amount, even if it was a few dollars too high. In fact, had my client been there, he would have said, "Gene, what's wrong with you? Get in the cab and don't waste your time worrying about getting beat out of five bucks."

But being cheated represented losing in what I perceived was a win-lose contest with the driver. It didn't even matter that this was a person I didn't know and who I'd never see again in my life. It didn't matter that I could have overpaid by fifty dollars and no one who knew me would ever know about it. I didn't want to lose and I wouldn't be persuaded to get in the cab until I convinced myself I wasn't going to lose.

As it turned out, I finally took a second cab for exactly the same fare, and I paid the same fare to return to the airport the next day. The fare the first driver quoted was the official fare. But even if it wasn't, I should have jumped in and gotten on with my business instead of wasting my time and energy. The worst part is that I knew it at the time. I knew all about the irrational anxiety that was stopping me from buying. Nevertheless, the anxiety that I would lose stopped me from making a simple decision that was in my best interests. Imagine the effect it can have on your Prospect when the win-lose issues at stake are more significant.

Perceived Cost

For everyone, life is a continual exercise in allocating limited resources. How much money, time, energy, personal risk, and emotion are we willing to expend in one activity instead of others; how much money to own one thing instead of something else; how much energy in one relationship instead of others? This running cost-benefit analysis that people go through trying to make the most of what they've got causes anxiety and stress. And when you ask to get your way, you almost always add to people's anxiety and stress, because whatever you're asking for almost always forces people to reallocate their money, time, energy, or support.

There's a tendency in selling to think of cost in terms of dollars, but in everyday life, money may not be the most important cost. Unless your boss owns the business, he doesn't personally pay your salary, so the dollar amount of your raise is financially irrelevant to him. Whether you earn 10 percent more or less has no effect on how much he has to spend on himself and his family. To your boss, the real costs of your raise, the things that will cause him buying anxieties, are the time, energy, and emotion he puts into dealing with you, other employees, his boss, and the human resources department.

Whatever your Prospect considers to be the cost of agreeing with you, the cost anxiety increases as he comes closer to making a decision. So, again, the negative force working against you gets stronger just as you're getting close to getting your way.

Despite the admitted importance of cost in many persuasion situations, it's blamed for more failed attempts at persuasion than it should be. When you demand a 10-percent raise, but your boss sticks at 8 percent, the issue may not be costs of any sort, but a need to win. If you've made the 10-percent raise a win-lose contest, his buying anxiety is a fear of losing, not a cost anxiety.

If you're interviewing for a new job, your high asking salary may have nothing to do with your not getting the job, even though that's the reason you're given. If your interviewers don't entirely trust you or believe you can do the job, the operative buying anxiety is their fear of making a mistake.

When costs are not the real issue, when they are just a lightning rod for one of the other four buying anxieties, it's essential to deal with the real buying anxieties your proposal is causing, not with the cost your Prospect is complaining about.

The lineup is complete, and it's five to one against.

Why People Don't Buy	*Why People Buy*
1. Reluctance to give up options 2. Fear of making a mistake 3. Social pressures 4. Fear of losing 5. High perceived costs	1. They believe that buying will fulfill their personal needs.

Your job is to reduce the conflict between the positive and negative buying forces and, in the end, to make the positive forces greater in your Prospect's mind than the negative ones.

Gentle Persuasion Habit No. 6

Be prepared to deal with people's five buying anxieties as they get closer to making a decision.

- *"But what about the options I'm giving up?"*
- *"Am I making a mistake by agreeing with you?"*
- *"How will I explain my decision to others?"*
- *"Am I going to come out of this a loser?"*
- *"Is this going to cost too much?"*

8

Easy-to-Buy

I AM THE WORLD'S WORST SALESMAN; THEREFORE, I
MUST MAKE IT EASY FOR PEOPLE TO BUY.

—F. W. Woolworth

There's a good chance that when it comes to getting your way in everyday life, you're your own worst enemy. Most people, Poets and professional salespeople alike, are.

It's more than just the tendency to focus on your interests instead of your Prospect's, and on situational needs instead of personal ones. Often the biggest problems start after your Prospect has subconsciously made the connection between what you're proposing and his needs, and is beginning to form the idea that it would be good for him to let you get your way.

At this point all that's left are his buying anxieties: the belief that he's forgoing valuable options, that he may be making a mistake, that people won't approve of his decision, that he may come out of the transaction a loser, or that it's not worth the cost. There are two ways to deal with these issues—the hard way and the easy way. Perversely, most people choose the hard way.

The Choice

The forces that keep people from buying even when they want to aren't forces of nature. They're caused by the very person they hurt the most—you. You set high prices, insist on retainers, write oppressive contracts. You're the employee who's argumentative and confrontational, the parent who sets up win-lose confrontations.

Once you've created buying anxieties, you then have to deal with them one at a time. This is the hard way of getting your way in everyday life.

The alternative is to structure your proposals so that buying anxieties don't become an issue in the first place. Then you don't have to work to overcome them. This defines "easy-to-buy."

When your proposal is easy-to-buy, you only have to be one-sixth as good a persuader as you have to be if you follow the conventional path. Instead of having to connect with the Prospect's personal needs *and* address the five buying anxieties, all you have to do is persuade people that you can meet their personal needs. If you're smart, the five buying anxieties that prevent people from buying can be so inconsequential that you barely have to address them.

Easy-To

In everyday life, easy-to-buy means being "easy-to": easy-to-do-business-with, easy-to-work-with, easy-to-deal-with, and easy-to-live-with. It means reducing to a minimum, or eliminating altogether, the anxieties that stop people from doing things you propose.

It sounds simple, but in practice most people aren't easy-to. They take up time and energy (high perceived costs), ask for commitments (loss of options), give uninformed opinions (low perceived competence leading to fear of making a mistake if their advice is followed), and boast of their personal successes and conquests (leaving the impression that their relationships with others are often win-lose situations). Too many people are hard-to people, not easy-to people.

A lawn services company I was considering sent me a multi-page complex contract committing me to a year's services. It set out provisions for what would happen if I failed to pay within thirty days and informed me I would be liable for attorney's fees not to exceed 25 percent of the invoices outstanding.

We're talking lawn-mowing here, not a strategic partnership to launch a manned space station. Although I wanted to hire the gardener, I didn't. I didn't want to commit for a year to someone with whom I had no previous experience (fear of making a mistake), and I didn't want to think through the possible consequences of the contract (fear of losing). The guy who ran the company was his own worst enemy. He lost my business by not being easy-to.

Being easy-to is not limited to small transactions in everyday life. A consulting firm I hired at a Fortune 200 company sent me a one-page-letter agreement that set out in simple English how we would work together to build a computer system. I didn't even have to sign and return the agreement. They were easy to do business with, and we spent $4 million with them.

I watched two young company vice presidents, Dave and Brendan, at a Fortune 100 company deal with the firm's cantankerous but brilliant founder, chairman, and autocratic leader. Both VPs were experienced, well educated, hardworking, opinionated, and aggressive, with a sharp intelligence that questioned every assumption, second-guessed every decision, and refused to accept the conventional wisdom.

Dave and Brendan were the same age, had attended business school together, were good friends, and had joined the company within a month of each other. Both sat on the company's executive committee, which approved investment proposals submitted by managers throughout the firm. They were thirty years younger than the chairman and his senior staff, and the chairman delighted in the modern new outlook the two brought to his company.

But Dave was a hard-to person and Brendan was an easy-to person. Dave's style was confrontational. Smarter, more articulate, and better educated in modern management principles than the older managers, he made every decision a win-lose contest. He delighted in demolishing older managers' proposals, leaving the managers looking foolish and incompetent in front of the chairman and his executive committee.

Although Dave was generally correct in his positions, he was hard to deal with. He wouldn't let up until he walked away from a conversation or meeting metaphorically holding his hands over his head like the winning boxer leaving the ring after a decisive knockout. He loved winning.

Brendan was the opposite. Although he, too, despaired of the moribund older managers and their ill-thought-out proposals, he was easy to deal with. Although he never backed down from a position he believed was right, he never turned issues into win-lose contests. He would try to persuade managers to change their proposals in private, before they came before the chairman and the executive committee. He always looked for positives in the original proposals, and offered suggestions and advice for changes, never challenges.

When a proposal he disagreed with came up in committee, his first words were usually to this effect: "First, I'd like you to know that I'll support whatever the committee decides on, and help to make it work." Then he'd find something positive to say about the proposal before presenting an alternate point of view. For example, "Bob is right that we have to fix the high downtime of packaging equipment in his department. He can't do his job the way things are now." Then he'd present his suggestion as a possible option that the committee might want to consider, not as the clear alternative to Bob's really dumb proposal.

The consequences of this difference between being hard-to and being easy-to were dramatic and swift. No one, not even the chairman, wanted to deal with Dave, even though his guidance was valuable and his suggestions almost always were adopted. Within a year he was asked to leave the company.

On the day Dave lost his job, Brendan was promoted and eventually went on to join the board of directors and become the company's second most powerful executive and the one most widely liked by everyone.

Like Dave and Brendan, managers, professionals, parents, teachers, and business heads make decisions every day that make them easy-to-deal-with or hard-to-deal-with. Without thinking, too often the choice is for hard-to-deal-with.

Poets typically respond to criticisms about not being easy-to by being defensive and reciting all the reasons why hard-to hurdles are necessary. Usually they involve protecting themselves from their Prospects or otherwise looking out for their own good.

"We'll lose our shirts on returns." "Warranty costs will kill us." "We'll be sued if we don't put these provisions in the contract." "I don't care if he is my boss, he was acting like a jerk and I couldn't let him go on without telling him what I thought." "I never talked back to my parents, and I'm not about to let you start talking back to me."

But if you really meet your Prospect's personal needs, you won't have to protect yourself from happy customers, employees, friends, or family members. Although you may occasionally get cheated or lose in a relationship, overall you'll win big. You'll get your way in everyday life more frequently, expending less energy and without infuriating your friends, clients, family, employees, or boss.

The Curse of Authority

The job of parent comes with an unfortunate perk: unquestioned authority for the first years of your child's life. It's unfortunate because for years you never have to lose any confrontation or bother explaining how your demands link to your child's personal needs. This gives you years to build a foundation that will make it nearly impossible for you to get your way once your reign of unquestioned authority is over.

If you're rigid, insisting on unnecessary structure and arbitrary obedience, children quickly learn you're not easy-to-deal-with. As they get older, they assert their own need to win, and themselves become difficult to deal with. Senseless skirmishes erupt around every issue, and life is miserable as parents and children fight a continuous battle to get their way.

None of this implies that important family decisions requiring experience, judgment, and wisdom should be bargained, negotiated settlements.* But in everyday life, it's not the life-and-death issues that dominate. If your daughter really dislikes pork chops and wants a tuna sandwich instead, agreeing will have no negative consequences on her upbringing, health, or moral values. Don't be difficult to deal with.

If your son wants to play with friends before doing his homework, it's worth a try before setting down arbitrary rules. If it doesn't work out, at least you'll have strong evidence you can use to explain your rules; you're not simply being difficult to deal with.

Save your persuasive ammunition for the important issues. Your children will see you as easy-to-deal-with, and won't feel that when you insist on certain points you're doing so simply because you always have to win.

Gentle Persuasion Habit No. 7

Be easy-to—easy-to-buy, easy-to-deal-with, easy-to-do-business-with, and easy-to-live-with.

---

*I am certainly not above using the force of parental authority when the issue is important enough and persuasion fails. For example, no amount of persuasion will get the trash cans routinely to our curb on trash night, and our indestructible plastic trash cans would decompose before the kids would bring them in without being forced to.

9

How People Buy

WE EVEN SELL A PAIR OF EARRINGS FOR UNDER £1,
WHICH IS CHEAPER THAN A PRAWN SANDWICH
FROM MARKS & SPENCER'S. BUT I HAVE TO SAY THE
EARRINGS PROBABLY WON'T LAST AS LONG.

—Gerald Ratner

You're in the middle of dinner when you get a call from a telemarketer selling subscriptions to *Poultry World* and *American Machine Gunner.* Twenty words into the sales talk, you bang the phone down and return to dinner, muttering epithets. The telemarketer was talking, but you weren't ready to listen. He didn't mentally connect. He was out of sync with his Prospect.

You're talking to your employees about the need to work seven days a week, sixteen hours a day, for the next six months, to rush out your product's next release. You're talking about situational needs—what the competition is doing, customers' demands, commitments you made to your boss—and asking them to consider an option that's not on their radar screen. They're thinking about personal needs—the start of summer, the planned family vacation, an elderly parent who needs daily attention, the Internet business they've started on the side. They're not thinking about what you're talking about. You're out of sync with your employees and not making the sale.

You've walked into a car dealership, still undecided whether you need an SUV, a station wagon, or a minivan. But the car salesman has latched onto you like a barnacle to a pier, and five minutes after shaking your hand he's telling you about dealer rebates and warranties, dealing with buying anxieties you don't yet have. He's out of sync with his Prospect, vibrating your eardrums but not communicating.

You're talking to your fourteen-year-old about his algebra grade, and he's asking you where in the real world is he ever in his entire life going to use quadratic equations, especially since he's going to start a band and become a rock star. He sees no personal need for algebra or a good grade in algebra, and you're not going to make the sale. You're out of sync with your Prospect.

In previous chapters we've talked about *why* people buy, and about situational needs, personal needs, and buying anxieties. We now need a simple model that describes how people sort out and deal with all this, and *how* they buy. Without this understanding, you're in danger of being out of sync with your Prospects, of talking about what they're not ready to listen to, of Talking Without Communicating.

The Buying Model

Although it doesn't always seem like it, buying is a remarkably rational process. Whenever people buy something, or you persuade people to do something, they go through the following five phases:

1. Awareness. Before people will even think about buying what you're selling, they must first believe they have unfulfilled needs, either personal or situational. More than that, they must believe there's some practical way to fulfill those needs with what you're selling. This is true if you're selling professional services to clients, aircraft carriers to the navy, your budget to your boss, or family values to your children. *Until this awareness occurs, there's no motivation to buy and no motivation to spend time or energy even considering buying.*

Any time you tell people about yourself, your ideas, or your products or services before they're aware they have needs that what you're selling can fulfill, you're just rattling eardrums. It's like the joke about trying to teach a pig to sing—you waste your time and annoy the pig.

That's what's happening in the algebra example. To most teenagers, becoming a rock-and-roll star means thousands of adoring fans, free money, and touring the country in a luxury bus chased by fanatic pubescent groupies. It's the ultimate fulfillment of a teenager's needs for recognition, wealth, independence, and sex. And you're talking about algebra. Unless you make him aware of how algebra and good grades can help him fulfill his personal needs, you're wasting your time and annoying your kid. In this situation you have two choices: Try to change his personal needs to ones that algebra and good grades can fulfill (good luck), or show him how algebra and good grades can fulfill the personal needs he does have.

My friend Mark was faced with this challenge when his ten-year-old son, Kevin, decided to form a band with his best friend and become a famous rock star. This happened after the boys saw the adulation the students in Kevin's school gave four classmates who wore sunglasses and played "Wild Thing" as a small part of a band concert.

Although this might just have been mildly amusing kid stuff, unfortunately Kevin also decided rock stars didn't have to care about good grades. Instead of arguing, Mark agreed with his son that becoming a famous rock star could be a good thing, because, he joked, famous rock stars always buy their parents luxury cars and expensive new houses.

But Mark pointed out that for Kevin's plans to succeed, it would probably be a good idea if the band members actually learned to play musical instruments. This, inconveniently, would mean music lessons, learning to read music, and practicing. Seeing the logic of this reasoning, Kevin used up a birthday wish to get an inexpensive guitar, and Mark found his son a guitar teacher.

Although Kevin did learn the first three chords of "Wild Thing," within a few weeks his dream of easily fulfilling his adolescent needs gave way to the reality of daily practice and having to work harder at music than he worked at school. It would be an exaggeration to say that this turned Kevin into a good student overnight—it didn't—but when Kevin realized rock and roll wasn't going to fulfill his needs, he did start listening to alternatives. He even listened to his father's suggestion that study and success at school could lead to personal satisfaction, acceptance by his peers, college, and the realistic fulfillment of many of his needs.

The good news was that within a year (yes, it took that long) Mark's son had, on his own, decided that doing well in school was important and raised his grades from C's and B's to A's. The guitar is gathering dust in the closet with Mark's Soloflex, but Mark and Kevin's relationship is stronger than ever.

2. Creating a short list. How do you deal with all the options that are open to you without going into systems overload? Very simply, you probably ignore entirely most of the options and concentrate on only a select few. At least that's what most people do.

Once people are aware that they have needs they can realistically fulfill, they create a "short list" of alternatives they're willing to consider. This list is not like the list you made for Santa when you were a kid, or the list you make before you head for the grocery store. Those are lists of nonexclusive choices you definitely want. A "short list" is a list of alternatives you'll consider, a list from which you'll make a single selection. Personal needs influence which options make the short list, but for the most part, situational needs prevail at this point.

At one point in my career I accepted a job in New York City and had to relocate from Chicago. Accepting the job made me aware of situational needs for a new home, so my wife and I turned our attention to fulfilling this need, not an easy task in New York City. There are more than a hundred towns that someone working in Manhattan can live in, starting with Manhattan and extending out to city and suburban communities in New York, New Jersey, and Connecticut.

We began our search by creating a short list of towns we'd consider, based on the length of the commute, on our preconceived notions of what the states and towns would be like, and on random conversations with helpful but not necessarily terribly knowledgeable friends and acquaintances. It didn't matter that we had never visited the towns we put on our short list and knew little or nothing about them. We needed a way of simplifying our search so we could complete it in a reasonable time. There were probably better homes than the one we finally bought, in communities we never visited, but because those neighborhoods didn't make our short list, we never considered them.

The most common reason people create a short list is to reduce to a manageable number the alternatives they have to research and consider. But people also create a short list to help them justify a decision they're predisposed to make. If your college-bound child is set on going to a school where he can spend his free time surfing, Harvard and the University of Vermont won't be on his short list, even if the reasons he gives you have nothing to do with surfing. Once they're not on the short list, he doesn't later have to come up with justifications for not choosing them.

This idea of a short list is important, because it's tough to persuade people to listen to options they haven't mentally included on their list. If your boss, for whatever reason, won't sponsor projects using unproven technologies, then he won't approve your proposal to reduce operating cost by replacing expensive Microsoft software with software your college buddy developed in his garage and is distributing free over the Internet. He won't even listen to you seriously.

Even though he knows he needs to reduce costs, your proposal hasn't made his short list. So if you're telling him how brilliant your buddy is, and waxing eloquent on the wonders of his software, you're wasting your time and annoying your boss. It's entirely irrelevant whether your proposal is good or bad, whether you're right or wrong. You're Talking Without Communicating.

3. Evaluating alternatives against situational needs. Once people are aware of needs and have a short list of alternatives they're willing to consider, the next step is evaluating the options on their list against their situational needs. In the case of our relocation search, my wife and I began by carefully looking at all homes that met our situational needs for bedrooms, location, affordability, and so forth.

In part, this is what Mark's son, Kevin, did in the year after his rock-star crisis. Without consciously thinking about it, he was evaluating his options—music, sports, fighter pilot, academics—before committing himself to a direction.

You do the same thing when you buy a new car. You begin with a list of makes and models you'll consider, and you evaluate those options against your situational needs. You eliminate the antique Jag you've always wanted because it won't provide reliable transportation. The Suburban won't fit into your garage. The Mercedes is too pricey. The Dodge minivan and Toyota station wagon stay because they'll hold your three kids and their stuff. If the salesperson wants to stay in sync with you, this is the time for him to be asking questions about how you'll use the car, what your budget is, and what you like and dislike about the different alternatives.

But the salesperson must not make the classic Poet mistake of thinking he's actually making the sale during this phase. It's true that by the time people are evaluating options on their short list against situational needs, they're well into the buying process. And this is the time they're most ready and willing to listen to all the good things you have to say about whatever it is you're selling. So he talks a blue streak, convinced he's making points, driving in the winning runs. Big mistake. All he's really doing, which is still important, is keeping himself in the running by not getting thrown off the short list. You're not ready to make the buying decision until the next phase.

4. Evaluating alternatives against personal needs. As soon as people understand how the different alternatives meet their situational needs, their attention turns to personal needs. This is where decision-making gets serious. If you're not in sync at this point, you're not going to get your way.

After my wife and I found several houses that met our situational needs, our emphasis shifted to personal needs—whether we could get a winning deal, the likelihood of appreciation (wealth), and something that might be summarized as the "prestige quotient" of the house, neighborhood, and town. We eventually chose a house that failed to meet several situational needs we thought were key: It didn't have a family room, it was short one bedroom, and it was priced above our budget. We had actually crossed it off our short list shortly after we first saw it.

But six months after we first looked at the house, in the dead of winter and during a severe housing recession, our agent suggested that the seller might accept an offer far below replacement cost. Bingo, the house moved to the top of our short list. The real-estate agent met our personal needs by finding an impressive home in the best town at a winning price. If she had stayed in the previous phase of the buying process, where we were evaluating alternatives against situational needs, she wouldn't have made the sale. But she stayed in sync with us, moving from situational needs to personal ones.

5. Resolving buying anxieties. As soon as people mentally make a buying decision, they're faced with all the buying anxieties the decision brings to the surface. Are they making a mistake? Are they going to come out of the transaction a loser? What will people think? Do they really want to give up other options? Can they afford it? Although it may not be apparent to you, by this point in the buying process, situational needs begin to have little influence on people's decisions. They come into play again only if your Prospect can't come to terms with her buying anxieties or can't figure out how to rationalize the alternative that best meets her personal needs.

The home my wife and I bought cost far more than we'd planned to pay, and thus failed to meet a situational need. But it was a great deal and met our personal need to win, as well as providing us with a perception of economic security (low downside risk) and possible wealth (high upside potential). It lacked several important amenities we wanted, again failing to meet situational needs. But it was an impressive home in one of the best New York City suburbs, and thus met our unspoken personal need for prestige and acceptance. We easily overcame our buying anxieties and justified buying the house.

Getting in Sync

When they're buying something, the employees, bosses, kids, clients, and anyone else in your everyday life are like post offices with five windows that are only open for business at certain times. The five windows can be characterized as follows: becoming aware of a need they can fulfill; making a short list; evaluating the purchase or idea against situational needs; evaluating it against personal needs; and, finally, working through their buying anxieties. If you hope to persuade people, they have to hear what you're saying, and they'll only hear you when you're standing in front of the correct open window and they're ready to listen. If you're at the wrong window at the wrong time, you may be talking, but the window is closed and you're not being heard.

To know which window is open, you have to listen to learn where people are in their buying process. Then you must react accordingly. If your Prospects are unaware of their personal needs, you must help them become aware before you can persuade them. If they're creating their mental short list, you should be working to be on it. If they're evaluating options against situational needs, you should be helping them evaluate your proposal. If they're evaluating options against personal needs, you should be demonstrating how your proposal will best meet their personal needs. If they're ready to commit, you must help them overcome their buying anxieties.

Consider the six-year-old facing a plate of carrots. This is a difficult persuasion situation, because the child is unaware of any needs he has that eating carrots can fulfill. It doesn't matter that you tell him he needs vegetables to grow up strong and healthy. He's gotten this far without carrots, and even though you have three college degrees and the kid still believes in the tooth fairy, you're not going to convince him he'll be three foot six for the rest of his life if he doesn't eat these exact carrots that happen to be in front of him on his specific plate right now. Because he doesn't like them, there's absolutely, positively no need those carrots can fulfill.

Now, parents instinctively recognize this challenge, so they create a need and make the child aware of it. "If you don't eat the carrots, you won't get dessert." If dessert is a big thing for the child, he suddenly becomes aware of a need he can fulfill by eating the carrots. You're in sync with his buying process by making him aware of a need that eating the carrots can fulfill before trying to persuade him to eat them.

Of course, this need is artificial. If your objective is to have your child eat well in the presence of the dessert police, fine. But you haven't succeeded in persuading your child to eat vegetables at school, or anywhere else where you're not hovering. To be truly persuasive, you should make your child aware of a legitimate need he really believes he has. (Hint: This is not something you're going to accomplish during one meal—maybe not even during one year, or during your entire lifetime. That being the case, don't fixate on one specific food. You're not with the United Carrot Council. What you're trying to sell is good nutrition, not carrots.)

On a more sophisticated level, consider a small law firm trying to win business from a new client. The client may be fully aware of her company's needs for legal advice, but if she's accustomed to retaining only larger, well-established firms, small firms like yours are not on her mental short list. Until you win a place on this list, the most enthusiastic description of your firm's experience and service orientation will fall on deaf ears.

So instead of talking about your partners' illustrious backgrounds and all your firm can do for her, you would be better served by not talking about your firm at all, but by persuading her of the advantages of adding a smaller firm to her approved counsel list, perhaps one specializing in practice areas that larger firms typically don't cover well.

Fixating on Cost

There's one mistake almost all of us make that cause us to get out of sync with our Prospects, that has us standing in front of a closed window, Talking Without Communicating. Not knowing where the Prospect is in his buying process, persuaders too often focus on buying anxieties before the Prospect has finished evaluating. And, more often than not, the buying anxiety they focus on is cost.

One reason people make this classic persuasion mistake is that so much emphasis is placed on price in the traditional selling that goes on in our lives. Radio, newspaper, and television advertising, department stores, discount stores, discount brokers, and the direct mail that floods our mailboxes all focus on price. Sales, limited-time offers, half-price specials, everyone bragging about the great deal they got. There's so much talk of price, it's easy for Poets to believe that it's the most important issue on people's minds.

In fact, it rarely is. Stay away from cost until you're absolutely certain that price is the buying anxiety your prospect is dealing with.

Janet is persuading her elderly mother, Margaret, to consider a nursing home, and cost is an important buying anxiety. Some options may be entirely unaffordable, and these will never make the short list. But once the options are reduced to an affordable few, it's best for Janet to put price aside to help her mother evaluate alternatives.

What's most important during the evaluation phase is that Margaret assess how the different options meet her situational and personal needs: proximity to family members and medical care, physical security, companionship with other residents. Only after this phase is complete, after her mother understands whether the facilities meet her needs, should Janet address buying anxieties, including cost. Keeping in sync with Margaret's natural buying phases makes buying less stressful for Margaret and persuasion more effective for Janet.

Gentle Persuasion Habit No. 8

Stay in sync with people's natural buying process. Talk about what they're prepared to listen to.

10

Good Examples

To ground the last chapters in everyday life, this one is devoted entirely to real-world examples. I've changed names and details to protect the innocent.

The Great Horse Trailer Caper

I recently found myself in the market for a horse trailer—an essential piece of gear, my daughter assured me, to support her equestrian ambitions. My personal knowledge of horses is limited to being able to differentiate, reasonably consistently and if I'm not standing too far away, between the animal's front and back ends. I know even less about horse trailers. Nevertheless, there I was at a horse trailer dealer on a Saturday morning, surrounded by different models of trailers from a single manufacturer, and talking to the flannel-shirted, cowboy-hatted, cowboy-boot-wearing owner and trailer salesman extraordinaire.

We quickly settled on a model with the features my daughter wanted, but I hesitated to buy. We knew the trailer we were considering would meet my daughter's needs, and it cost significantly less than I had steeled myself for when we started the great trailer search. Rationally, I should have done the deal and gotten on with the weekend. What was stopping me from buying?

First, I was afraid of making a mistake. I knew nothing about other manufacturers' models. I was worried that this low-cost trailer's quality, reliability, and safety might turn out to be poor, and that I should buy a "better" trailer, even though I didn't know what made one trailer better than another.

The salesman convincingly dealt with this buying anxiety by factually comparing the construction of competing trailers in a way that was credible and that established his brand's quality in my engineering-trained mind. While there were differences among brands, I felt that I wasn't losing anything important by going with his lower-priced trailer.

The second buying anxiety holding me back was a fear of losing. Like most people, I don't want to pay the asking price if even one other person on earth paid less. Face it—if you learn that someone, anywhere, paid less, you feel like a loser. If you learn you got a better deal than someone else, you feel as if you've won. The salesman understood this, and the way he dealt with price was nothing short of brilliant.

When I offered to pay less than the asking price (not because I thought it was worth less, or it was more than I had planned to pay, but simply because I didn't want to lose), his response was, "We're the largest dealer in the area and buy so many from the factory every month that we sell at absolutely the lowest price."

So far, this is more or less what you'd expect any salesperson to say, and there's no particular reason to believe it. But then he said, "I'll give you my customer list. If you can find one person who paid even five dollars less than the asking price for any trailer we've sold since we opened over ten years ago, I'll give you the trailer for free." That was good enough for me. We did the deal.

Our situational needs and the features and cost of the trailer itself ceased to be factors in my decision early on. If the salesman had droned on about the wonders of the actual trailer, I would have left to comparison-shop. But he instinctively understood that I was afraid of making a mistake and that I was worried about losing. He addressed both buying anxieties head-on and credibly.

I referred to the man who sold me the trailer as a salesman, but in fact he was a Poet. If he had had even a day of formal sales training, which I doubt, he certainly didn't show it. Not once did he resort to classic selling tactics. If he had, I'd have bolted, and he wouldn't have made the sale. Like most people, I really, really hate forced-persuasion selling, and I know immediately when I'm the target of a smooth-talking, traditional, manipulative salesperson. But this was just a good old boy who was so far from smooth that he couldn't have reached it on the Concorde without refueling twice. Yet he sold me his trailer even though he was the first dealer I visited, and I'd walked onto his lot with no intention of buying without doing extensive research.

All he did was exactly what you can do when you're trying to get your way with your boss, client, child, or spouse. He listened and he stayed perfectly in sync with me as I went through my buying process. He didn't talk about price until after I'd gone though the evaluation phases, and when I finally brought up cost, he understood that the dollar price wasn't my real buying anxiety; it was fear of losing. He never talked without communicating.

The Underdog Wins

A Fortune 100 company asked four executive recruiting firms to bid on a search for a chief information officer (CIO). Two were major players in executive recruiting, with nationwide practices and superb reputations. The third was a well-known boutique specializing in technology-oriented searches. The fourth was Fred, a Poet and newcomer with absolutely no experience, no employees, and no track record.

Price wasn't a factor. All executive recruiters charged the same fees, with no one in the industry discounting, so the chance of the customer's looking like a loser by overpaying wasn't an issue.

All four firms met on the same day with the vice president of human resources and the chief financial officer, to whom the CIO would report. The objective was for each firm to present its qualifications and persuade the Prospect to choose its proposal. The sellers were all Poets, and *all proposals were for the exact same service at exactly the same price.*

The three established search firms made the classic Poet selling mistake. They spent their time eloquently describing their product—themselves. They talked about their partners' experience, the breadth of their contacts and candidate databases, their reputations and their success with similar searches. They were all impressive firms with impeccable qualifications.

Fred took a different approach altogether. His qualifications were wanting. He had no candidate database, and this would be his first executive search assignment. All he had going for him was a background in computer technology; previously he had been both a CIO and a technology consultant. On every measure—experience, staff, references, resources, contacts— Fred was hopelessly outgunned. He was only in the running at all because of a mistake by the CEO. Fred, as he later readily admitted, was in way over his head.

Instead of talking about himself, his firm, and his experience, which would have been a short conversation in any case, he spent thirty of his allotted forty-five minutes asking questions about the company's technology strategy and the challenges facing the new CIO. He let the other guy talk first.

For the last fifteen minutes, Fred directed his comments to the CFO. He described his understanding of the CFO's needs and the qualifications the CIO would have to possess to fulfill them. Whether knowingly or instinctively, Fred directly addressed the CFO's needs to reduce his personal risk, to be accepted by his peers (the users), and to win. *He never talked about his own qualifications as a recruiter,* if for no other reason than that he had none. He helped the CFO visualize his needs being fulfilled by vividly describing different CIOs whom Fred knew personally and who might have the right qualities for success.

He won the assignment. The competitors were stunned that someone with no experience in big-time executive search could beat them. But Fred did what the self-centered pros didn't have the instinct to do. Instead of talking about himself, he listened to his Prospect's personal needs and then helped him visualize how he could fulfill them.

Got Milk?

My daughter dislikes milk as passionately as my dog dislikes the UPS truck. It's as useless to talk to her about how important milk is in supplying calcium, vitamin D, and protein to growing girls as it is to talk to my dog about how much we appreciate the stuff the UPS driver delivers. We've come to accept this, but we're concerned nevertheless because she's a light eater, and it's difficult finding a substitute for milk.

For years we fought an uphill battle, always worried that she wasn't getting the calcium needed by an active growing girl. Actually, this isn't accurate. We worked hard not to fight a battle, never to turn food into a win-lose situation. Instead we tried a series of calcium-rich products like yogurt, cheeses, calcium-fortified orange juice, and even ice cream. But we always considered this merely a holding action until we could persuade her to make the right choices on her own.

We did this by continuing to educate her about nutrition and the personal needs that good nutrition met for her. These were not abstract needs she might have far into the future, like a long life or healthy children of her own. We concentrated instead on needs she already had—to be tall, to have attractive teeth, and to be in good physical condition.

For years our message didn't connect, falling on the ears of a child who, like many children raised in America today, can't relate to anything personally negative. But at around eleven or twelve, which is still young, things slowly changed. She began to accept the proof we provided her, which was in the form of studies and news articles. She became aware that good nutrition could fulfill compelling personal needs.

She began to ask us about the nutritional content of different foods, making her own short list of foods she considered good for her and that she was willing to eat. She tried everything, and finally settled on a diet she correctly believed was a healthy one. (Well, close enough.) She still doesn't particularly care for everything she eats, but she makes her own choices, which are good ones, and we no longer worry about what she eats. Now *she* worries about what she eats, because we made the sale for good nutrition.

This is a sale we would never have made if we hadn't had the patience to wait until my daughter became aware of her own personal needs and how good nutrition could fulfill them. Being both a typically neurotic parent who worries about even the smallest aspects of my children's upbringing and someone who is personally health-conscious, I can tell you that it wasn't easy to bite my tongue, not bark out orders, not resort to rewards and punishments. But I knew my parents were never successful in getting me to eat Brussels sprouts when I was a child (I secretly fed them to our dog under the table, which proves, if nothing else, that dogs will eat anything), so I was living proof that this forced-persuasion approach didn't work.

Dogbreath

Although it took years to persuade my daughter, sometimes you get lucky and results are more immediate. When I used a similar gentle-persuasion strategy with my son, I moved things in the right direction in less than five minutes. The challenge was to persuade a ten-year-old to brush his teeth, which he would never do unless he was told. Never.

One morning when I went to his room to wake him for school, I got a good whiff of his morning breath. I fell off his bed and rolled on the floor, clutching my throat. "Dogbreath alert, dogbreath alert," I moaned. "It's too late for me, but save yourself," I shouted downstairs to my wife. To my son I said, in a tortured whisper, "My final words to you, the wisdom a father passes down to his only son, the words I hope you pass on to your son, are these: Don't breathe on anyone in school before you brush your teeth." Then I twitched one final time and died.

Of course he knew I was kidding, and he laughed the way you'd expect a normal ten-year-old to laugh at stupid Dad-type antics. But he also knew I wasn't kidding about his breath. And he was at an age where acceptance by the kids in his class was an important personal need. We only rarely have to remind him to brush his teeth now, especially on school days. Amazing.

Welcome to the Family

We now turn from a real family to one created by a motorcycle company, in what has got to rank as one of the most effective examples of the power of addressing personal needs in selling.

Fewer than 3 percent of licensed drivers in the United States own motorcycles, but those who do are passionate about it. Unlike owning a car, owning a motorcycle, at least in the United States, is never just an issue of satisfying the situational need of having to get from one place to another. For the most part, cars do a better job.

Despite the passion of its customers, however, the motorcycle industry exemplifies the futility of building a selling strategy based on product superiority. A constant stream of marginal innovations and improvements over the past forty years has dramatically changed the basic product. But from year to year the average consumer, who is neither a motorcycle expert nor a mechanical engineer, is hard pressed to tell who's truly ahead.

But anyone who knows anything about motorcycles knows that for at least forty years before 1999, Harley-Davidson never produced a superior product.* Japanese and German motorcycles especially were more reliable and more technically advanced, handled and performed better than Harleys, and cost significantly less.

Nevertheless, for years, Harley-Davidson dealers sold out of nearly all models, with most selling at 10 percent to 30 percent above list. Most competing, "superior" motorcycles sold at a discount from already lower list prices. In the United States the single best-selling model from any manufacturer in 1998 and 1999 was the Harley-Davidson Fat Boy, at the time (before the 2000 models) arguably one of the poorest-handling, most uncomfortable, most overpriced motorcycles sold in the free world. Yet dealers sold out, and many customers waited more than a year for delivery while superior motorcycles gathered dust in competitors' showrooms. How could this happen?

There's not one single reason for Harley-Davidson's success, but one part is the Harley Owners Group (H.O.G.), created

---

*If you're a Harley owner and enthusiast, save your stamps. Before 1999, Harley-Davidson made fine products, but it didn't make the best products. With the 1999 and 2000 models, an argument can be made that all that has changed. What hasn't changed, however, is Harley's understanding of its customers' personal needs, which is second to none.

by Harley-Davidson exclusively for Harley owners. H.O.G. sponsors motorcycle safety training, group rides, rallies, and charity events. H.O.G. events, from local one-day rides to major national rallies, attract from fifty local riders to more than 400,000 motorcyclists from around the world.

The most interesting dynamic, from a sales standpoint, is the number of owners who have centered their social lives around H.O.G. and Harley-Davidson. For these people, acceptance by H.O.G. and other Harley-Davidson owners is an important motivation for purchasing Harley-Davidson branded clothing, accessories, and motorcycles. This is underscored by a video-tape that Harley buyers receive with their purchase of a new motorcycle. The tape is titled *Welcome to the Family.*

This need for acceptance is powerful stuff. A Harley owner once admitted to me that she'd like to buy a BMW motorcycle, which she test-drove and found to be more comfortable, more responsive, and easier to handle than her 1998 Harley. But she was afraid riders who rode Harleys wouldn't accept her.

Now, we're talking about an intelligent, college-educated, professional woman here, and the other riders she was referring to *were not even people she knew.* They were strangers she'd pass on the road or briefly talk to at motorcycle rallies.

Harley-Davidson is not alone in appealing to a personal need for acceptance. IBM, the Saturn division of General Motors, real-estate developers, country clubs, fashion designers, and drug dealers use the same persuasion strategy. It's a strategy that centers around an important personal need, and only peripherally involves the product.

Interestingly, the same need for acceptance is at work in society as a whole, though in some societies more so than others. The Confucian-influenced East Asian societies, such as Japan, China, and Korea, set out clear standards for acceptance by the society at large and by smaller groups within it, such as schools, neighborhoods, and businesses. Acceptance by the group is so important to most people in these societies that it is the most potent force persuading people to conform to societal norms. It's widely believed that this high need for acceptance by the group is the reason for the far lower crime rates in East Asian countries compared with the United States, which places a higher value on individualism than on group acceptance.

Effective parents all over the world use this same need for acceptance within their families as a way of encouraging acceptable behavior. They set standards of morality and behavior through their teachings and through the example of their own behavior, and they accept nothing less from their children. While children in these cohesive families don't fear being thrown out in the streets for behavior that doesn't meet their parents' standards, they know they'll lose the warm acceptance and approval of their family members for behavior that falls short. In these families, the need for acceptance has a far more persuasive influence on family members' behavior than do all outside influences combined.

A High-Tech Lesson

I learned the power of easy-to-buy when I was running a high-tech software firm. As an undercapitalized startup, we were always strapped for cash, so we watched every purchase. The habit continued even after we were a $100-million company.

One day in the course of conversation with the product developers, I learned we'd spent over $200,000 on a software product to use in our own R&D efforts. I was flabbergasted.

The company's executive committee, which I chaired, reviewed every purchase above $5,000, and we prided ourselves on how tight-fisted we were. Furthermore, independent of cost, we never made a decision that committed us to an important or irrevocable direction without first talking about it. Yet in less than two years we spent $200,000, without my knowledge, for a product that became such an integral part of our product-development process that we were totally dependent on it.

This was the result of smart salesmanship on the part of the vendor who sold us the software. It had made its product so easy to buy that we did buy it.

First, it packaged the product so that unit prices of different components were less than $1,000. This was lower than the lowest purchase price of competing products, and low enough for most technical people to buy without management approval. Although the total we spent for the product was high, the *perceived* costs were so low that they were not an issue, even for a company that watched every dollar.

The product was also easy-to-buy because the vendor didn't position it as "strategic." It's especially popular for high-tech vendors to call their products strategic, because they believe that strategic products are important products, and if their products are important—well, then, the vendor and its employees must be important.

What this strategy fails to consider is that important products are hard-to-buy, while unimportant products are easy-to-buy. It's like the difference between buying a tank of gas and buying a new car.

Even though this software product became an integral part of our operations and was in fact strategic, the vendor sold the product as a low-cost way to solve a common problem. There was never the sense that our company was giving up other options. Consequently, we never went through the time, energy, and hand-wringing that makes buying important products so time-consuming.

It was no big deal. It was easy-to-buy.

I should emphasize that the vendor in no way misrepresented its product. We chose to buy $200,000 worth of it and made it strategic because it turned out to be a good product, not because we were tricked. It was the right decision. But if it hadn't been easy-to-buy, we would have pondered, analyzed, and argued the decision, and perhaps gone in a different direction.

Winning Hearts

What we see from these examples is that persuasion isn't just for salespeople, and that, although it must be deliberate, it can be far from what most people think of as selling. But an even more important lesson is that your relationships can improve when you're persuasive in the right way. You can win people's hearts while you win their minds.

I only know one horse trailer salesperson. I genuinely like him and recommend him to my daughter's friends' parents. This wouldn't have been the case if he hadn't listened to me so well and understood and answered my needs and anxieties.

Fred, the recruiter, went on to have a close business and personal relationship with his first client that lasted for decades. In fact, his client became his friend and the godfather of one of his children.

The jury's still out on how my children will finally get along with us, but right now we're in the teenage years everyone tells me are supposed to be so terrible, and they're wonderful. My children are becoming strong, independent young people without the rebellion that's so destructive in many families. I like to think the reason is that Deborah and I haven't given them anything to rebel against, no ongoing contest of wills that they have to win to develop into independent adults. Like sheepdogs, we've tried to keep them moving in the right direction, but as long as they're reasonably in the herd, we don't dictate their every step.

Harley-Davidson has a higher percentage of happy customers than any other company I know. I've never talked to a Harley owner who said anything seriously negative about the company or its products. On the contrary, I have watched owners emotionally defend obvious product faults against owners of "rice burners" (a pejorative term that nearly all Harley owners use when talking of Japanese motorcycles) and experts in the motorcycling press. All it takes for any publication to ensure that the editor is deluged with angry letters questioning the intelligence, patriotism, and manhood of an author is an article that compares Harley-Davidson motorcycles unfavorably with Japanese or European products.

The company has had a tumultuous history, and it's taken decades to finally fix serious product shortcomings. But the company persuades by listening to its customers and fulfilling their personal needs, not through massive advertising (for years Harley-Davidson spent exactly zero on advertising) and hard-sell tactics (customers plead to get an available bike assigned to them). The result is customers who love the company and its products with a passion other companies can only envy.

That persuaders' relationships in the examples above were strengthened even as they worked to get their way shouldn't be surprising. People are drawn to people who listen to them, figure out what they need, and sincerely work to fulfill these needs. After all, this is what your mother did when you were a baby and a toddler, and your response was unconditional love.

Shifting your attention from what you're selling to your Prospect's personal needs and buying anxieties entirely changes the way you go about getting your way in everyday life. But eventually you have to persuade people that what you're selling meets their personal needs better than other options available to them. You must get them to believe you or they won't be able to resolve their buying anxieties.

Knowing why and how people buy, what they're thinking, and what motivates and worries them takes you a long way toward getting your way in everyday life and improving your relationships, but it's not enough. You still have to be persuasive. That comes next.

Step 2

Be Credible

11

The Magic Selling Formula

WOULD YOU BUY A USED CAR FROM THIS MAN?

A lawyer you're consulting comes to your meeting late and shabbily dressed, stares out the window while he's talking to you, and mumbles answers to your questions. Despite three advanced degrees and a colleague's referral, somehow the lawyer's not credible and it's no sale. You end the meeting intent on finding someone else to represent you.

A programmer you're consulting comes to your meeting late and shabbily dressed, stares out the window while he's talking to you, and mumbles answers to your questions. Although he has the same personal characteristics as the lawyer you didn't hire, you find the programmer credible. You agree to an outrageous consulting fee and follow his advice to the letter.

Your new manager is a notorious rogue, obviously out for himself, with no clue about the function he's responsible for managing. You know he's incompetent and untrustworthy, and nothing he says can persuade you to stay in his department.

The salesman selling you the Mercedes is an obvious rogue,

doesn't know cars, will receive a fat commission if you buy, and clearly doesn't care if you fall off the edge of the earth after your check clears. You know he's incompetent and untrustworthy, yet he persuades you to buy a new car from him instead of from someone you've known for years because he's willing to sell it for a thousand dollars less.

In this part of the book, we'll look at how you and all the personal things about you—things like what you know, your appearance, and how you dress—affect your persuasiveness. As the examples above demonstrate, the relationship between the personal characteristics of the persuader and persuasiveness is not always straightforward or consistent. Two different people can dress or act the same way in two different situations and the results can be exactly the opposite, in one case positive and in another negative. In one situation your personal characteristics may be important and in another entirely irrelevant.

Although the linkage between your personal characteristics and your persuasiveness is not as simple as it might at first appear, or as simple as conventional wisdom would lead us to believe, we can't forget that we're Poets here. As enlightened amateurs of persuasion, we want the simplest effective solution, not one that's so detailed we can't easily use it in our everyday lives.

Well, the simplest solution is simple indeed: *You must be credible—believable—to be persuasive.* This only stands to reason, for, after all, people will never do what you ask if they can't believe what you say. But what is it that makes us credible, and how do we become credible without a complete personal makeover?

Although we'll look at how twelve different personal characteristics affect your persuasiveness, we're going to pay special attention to the big three that most affect your credibility: your perceived competence, your trustworthiness, and the extent to which you seem to put other people's interests at least equal to your own. These three are almost always critical to getting your way. All others, such as the first impression you make, how likable you are, your appearance, and the way you dress, are important sometimes and unimportant at other times.

We're going to devote a separate chapter to each of the big three, but we can't entirely ignore the lesser personal characteristics altogether. In particular, we need to understand the *apparently* inconsistent influences that different personal characteristics have on persuasiveness under different circumstances.

In fact, people are not as inconsistent as they first appear. Persuasion research has unraveled the apparent inconsistencies by distinguishing between two different kinds of persuasion issues: those that are important to the person being persuaded and those that aren't.

Is This Really Important to Me?

Whether a decision is important depends on your point of view. To many people, which of two similar candidates is elected president of the United States is unimportant. Politically active and aware citizens, on the other hand, perceive it to be very important. To most people the brand of sneakers they wear is unimportant. But it's important to serious runners.

As it turns out, there's a big difference between what influences people's beliefs and decisions on issues they consider important and on issues they feel aren't. Specifically:

On issues people feel are unimportant, your persuasiveness is strongly influenced by your personal characteristics—the way you dress, your appearance, your voice, and your handshake. For example, people with little interest in politics tend to be most influenced by a candidate's appearance and style.

If you're running for secretary of your homeowners' association, your personal characteristics will probably carry the day. Even though homeowners vote, who becomes secretary will have no effect on their lives. It's not important to them. They don't bother carefully listening to and analyzing facts, position statements, and opinions, because it's not worth their time and energy. Life is complex enough without sweating the small stuff.

On issues people feel are important, they may initially be influenced by your personal characteristics, but will ultimately form their beliefs and make their decision based on the strength of your arguments and supporting evidence. They'll factor in your personal characteristics only if they're relevant to the central issue.

If you're trying to persuade your neighbors to approve a community project that will cost them each a lot of money, it won't matter that you're attractive, well dressed, and the president of a Fortune 500 company; they'll be most persuaded by the force of your arguments explaining how much the project will cost them and how it will meet their needs.

As far as your personal characteristics go, your neighbors may take your appearance, demeanor, and position as evidence of your competence, which would help you make your case. Or they may take those same personal characteristics as evidence that you probably don't understand the financial constraints of people with more limited means and vote against you.

The same thing happens when you interview for a job. The interviewer is influenced by both the evidence you provide that you can meet her needs and by only those personal characteristics that are relevant to the job. If you're applying for a legal position, relevant personal characteristics may be your appearance, intelligence, and trustworthiness. But if you're applying for a programming job, your appearance may be irrelevant.

All this is comforting, because it says that people make decisions rationally. If something isn't important, they don't spend time and energy analyzing and thinking about it. They focus on the persuader. Sometimes they make bad choices, but there's too much to do and think about in life to study every little decision. On the other hand, if something is important, people are influenced by your personal characteristics only if they're relevant to what they're buying.

It's a Wonderful Life

Despite the different weights people give your personal characteristics in different circumstances, there is a magic formula for persuasion. Very simply: Be competent, be trustworthy, and put other's interests first.

This is ethical persuasion that doesn't depend on tricks and manipulation. The formula works because competence, trustworthiness, and a sincere desire to fulfill others' needs are the three personal characteristics that most positively affect your credibility. If you embrace these three core values, gentle persuasion is easy.

To me, an ideal model of these values is George Bailey in the classic movie *It's a Wonderful Life*, which I watch with my family every Christmas season. George has a family, a struggling business, friends, competitors, enemies, and dreams and aspirations. He's an ordinary person living among ordinary people—some competent and some not, some well-meaning and supportive and others not. In other words, he's a lot like you and me.

The movie follows George from public school through marriage, raising a family, and taking over his father's small-town bank. What's wonderful about the movie is the portrayal of the hero as just an average person whose only real advantages in life, his trademarks from childhood to adulthood, are his core values. He's competent and trustworthy, and has a sincere interest in others that makes him consistently put other people's needs ahead of his own.

Throughout his life, these core values win him the support of everyone who knows him. Then George reaches a crisis in his life. The town bad-guy and scrooge, Mr. Potter, in an effort to take over George's bank, steals the bank's money and throws the blame on George. He accuses George of gambling, drinking, and womanizing, and calls in the bank auditors and the sheriff.

George is helpless, but his wife turns to the townspeople. A lifetime of competence, trustworthiness, and putting others' needs first pays off. Ignoring the apparent evidence against him, the town responds immediately and overwhelmingly, with everyone making personal sacrifices to help George out. Even the bank auditors and the sheriff contribute. And it happens without George's making a single sales call or presentation and without calling in favors. In the end, good triumphs over evil and George and the bank are saved. (Now, is this a great movie or what?)

Although George and his story are fictional, the underlying truth of the story isn't. People who adopt the three core values prevail in their lives. They win people's minds and hearts. As you read the rest of this book, remember George Bailey.

The Three-Step Plan
STEP 2: Be Credible.

In the next three chapters we'll look at the three core values of competence, trustworthiness, and putting others' interests first. Then we'll look at other personal characteristics that have much less influence on your persuasiveness, especially if what you're proposing is important to the person you're persuading. These characteristics include the impression you make when someone first meets you, your appearance, dress, body language, handshake, and personal trademarks, whether you're liked, and your similarity to your Prospect. We'll talk about these in a separate chapter, and clear up some common misconceptions.

12

Competence

THE LEADER MUST KNOW, MUST KNOW THAT
HE KNOWS, AND MUST BE ABLE TO MAKE IT
ABUNDANTLY CLEAR TO THOSE ABOUT HIM
THAT HE KNOWS.

—*Clarence B. Randall*

Persuasion research is unequivocal on few points, but one is that your competence, or at least the perception of it, makes a difference. If people believe you're competent, you're more likely to persuade them *in both important and unimportant matters.*

Perceived competence is the listener's belief that you know what you're talking about. When you're persuading people, they listen to what you say about how your proposal will fulfill their needs, how much it will cost, why it's better than others, and why they won't be making a mistake to accept it. They can't have confidence in what you say if they don't believe you know your stuff. So the more competent you appear to them, the more persuasive you'll be. It only makes sense.

When I was the CEO of a startup software company, I found that I was very persuasive within the company on issues dealing with sales and marketing. But when it came to getting my way in areas dealing with technology, it was an uphill battle.

The reason was simple. For the three years before we formally launched the company and for a year after, I did all the marketing, made every sale, and raised all the financing. As far as the company's technical people were concerned, the results were all the proof they needed that I was a sales and marketing expert. That perception made me very persuasive in these areas, and I had no trouble getting my way there.

But it was a very different story when it came to technology. To the technical staff it didn't matter that I had taught computer science early in my career or, at another time, had been the senior executive responsible for managing a number of advanced technology groups with annual budgets exceeding $100 million. I had never been a programmer. I hadn't worked my way up through the programming ranks. Therefore the product developers thought it was impossible for me to be technically competent.

To say I wasn't persuasive on technology issues within my own company is an understatement. Any opinions I expressed on technology that hadn't yet received the blessing of the company's chief technology officer were ignored. In retrospect, this may have been a good thing, but at the time it was occasionally a source of frustration.

This contrasted sharply with my persuasiveness with customers, who were senior technology executives in large organizations. Because I had once held the same job they were in, and then had become the head of a successful high-tech company, they considered me to be especially competent in technology. Consequently I was very persuasive on technology issues with customers, often even more persuasive than the product developers. At meetings, customers would turn to me for my opinions and agreement before they'd accept what product developers would tell them. This was frustrating to the product developers, and, I'm not ashamed to admit, gratifying to me.

The point is that my technical competence was whatever it was. But I was persuasive with the group who perceived me to be competent and unpersuasive with the group who perceived that I was not competent.

The same relationship between perceived competence and persuasiveness holds true in all aspects of everyday life. You will be persuasive with your spouse, children, parents, and friends in areas where they consider you to be competent. Your parents will take your advice on what computer to buy if you work for a high-tech company and what stock to buy if you work for a stockbroker. You may work in the mailroom and know little about computers or investing, but it's the perception of your competence that makes you persuasive.

This helps explain why well-dressed retail salespeople sell more high-fashion clothing than those who aren't well dressed. You look at them and you believe, before they say a single word, that they understand fashion. Because you interpret appearance as an indication of fashion competence, when a chic saleslady says, "It's you, it's you," you're more likely to believe her than if she were frumpy.

What If You're Not Exactly Competent?

Life would be a lot easier if everyone thought you were an expert in everything. But you're not, and in everyday life, as well as in business life, you often have to be persuasive in areas where you're not perceived as especially competent.

You run the human resources department and you have to convince your boss to increase your department's budget. Your boss considers you an expert in running the human resources function, but doesn't believe you know how to manage a budget. Trouble ahead.

You're applying for a job as a programmer, but have an

undergraduate degree in history. Trouble ahead. It doesn't matter that you've wasted your youth in learning programming and have more natural technology skills than most computer science graduates. The interviewer doesn't believe you're as competent as his other candidates, even though you are.

You're trying to persuade your kids to eat healthy foods, but you're overweight and out of shape. Trouble ahead. Your kids may be preteens, and rational thought to them is still a novel concept, but somehow they know you're not exactly competent to be giving advice on health and nutrition. So don't be surprised that you're not persuasive.

Your marriage is a disaster and you're advising your daughter to drop her emotionally abusive boyfriend. Trouble ahead? Maybe, or maybe not. If your daughter views your marriage as evidence that you're not competent in the area of relationships, you won't be persuasive.

But if your relationship with her is good, and you've talked to her about what you learned from your own marriage, she's more likely to see your marriage problems as evidence of your competence—as hard-won, painful experience.

You're the youngest partner in a professional firm—a lawyer, investment banker, or portfolio manager. Or you're the youngest editor on staff, or a new literary agent, or a doctor fresh out of medical school. You may have graduated summa and have a 160 IQ, but there's a good chance your perceived competence won't be as high as that of people you're competing with, simply because you have less experience. Trouble ahead.

There are three ways to deal with low perceived competence: become competent, change people's perception of your competence, or team up with someone who is competent. Not all three work in every situation, and not all three are always easy to pull off. But the one absolute is that you'll never be persuasive if people think you're not competent, so you've got to do something.

Get Competent

If people expect you to be competent, but you don't really know what you're talking about, sort of making it up as you go along and faking your way through, the chances are that you're not fooling anyone. Sooner or later, and usually it's way sooner than you think, people catch on and your persuasiveness sinks to zero.

The good news is that if you really can become competent, you almost automatically become more persuasive. So stop being lazy; get competent.

If the issue with your kids is nutrition, do some research, read studies, become genuinely as competent as you need to be, and share what you learn with your children. Stop wolfing down Chee-tos and Krispy Kremes and raiding the Halloween candy. It doesn't matter how young they are, eventually they'll understand nutrition is an area you're competent in and slowly you'll be able to persuade them.

If you're the youngest member on staff and, despite 800's on your SATs and your Phi Beta Kappa key, you really don't have any practical experience, go out and get it. It often takes remarkably little experience to increase your competence enormously. Work on the shop floor on third shift for a few weeks, ask to go out on sales calls, or sit on the phones in customer service for an hour a day for a few weeks. Read manuscript evaluations done by experienced editors or agents, buy and use competing products.

If the issue is your lack of knowledge, read books, take courses, study, and ask questions—learn. But, whatever you do, don't pretend to know more than you do, which is an unfortunate disease people who become partially competent are susceptible to. It doesn't matter that you may know more than the people you're talking to. As soon as you start to fake it, people catch on that you're talking through your hat and you'll be labeled as both incompetent and, even worse, untrustworthy. It can be a label you'll never remove.

So even if people expect you to be an expert and you're working hard at being competent, admit when you don't know something. People expect you to be competent, not omniscient. If you really are competent, people will give you some slack, time to look things up, consult with others, or otherwise come up with answers. But if you fake it and you're caught, the deal's off. They may never again believe anything you say, even if you really are competent.

Changing Perceptions

Of course, it's possible that you're competent but people don't know it. While this certainly happens, it doesn't happen as often as people think. More frequently, people who are perceived as incompetent are in fact incompetent.

But like the history graduate who could program, any parent of a teenager, or the brilliant young professional, it's entirely possible that you're more competent than your Prospects believe you are. If this is the case, your challenge is an easy one. You only need to change people's perceptions by proving your competence.

At one point in my career I was made the general manager of a food processing business that did $1.4 billion in sales per year. One staff member I inherited was Willie, the head of quality control, unquestionably one of the most important jobs in the division.

All I knew about Willie was that he was twenty-eight, single, and movie-star handsome, with Tom Selleck hair and a bushy mustache, and seemed to divide his free time between dating and hunting. He looked very much like a 1960s folk singer and not at all like an executive who managed several hundred people responsible for assuring that we never gave even a single one of our hundreds of thousands of customers food poisoning.

I started my new job stupidly predisposed to question

Willie's competence, fully expecting I'd have to replace him and correct what I was reasonably sure was a mistake on the part of my predecessor. This same sort of mindless prejudice is inflicted every day on thousands of people—often minorities, women, the disabled, people who graduated from the wrong school, or speak with an accent—people who are in any way different from whatever the norm happens to be in the situation.

In this case it took less than an hour during our first meeting to change my perceptions. It turned out Willie had two college degrees from one of the country's top agricultural colleges, was passionate about product quality, and knew every nook and cranny in the plant and every detail of the manufacturing process.

We'll talk about ways to change people's perception of your credibility in chapters 19 and 20. But as Willie showed, it's not that tough. If you're really competent, it's easy to get your competence to shine through, and you don't have to be a super salesperson to do it.

Team Competence

We live in a time when it's not only impossible to be competent in everything, it's not even possible to be competent in everything people expect us to be competent in.

I've seen the credibility of top corporate lawyers who advise the largest companies in the world on the most complex issues discredited by venture capitalists and twenty-something company founders because the lawyers didn't understand the financing, intellectual property, and cultural issues of small high-tech companies.

I've seen a man running a small business entirely disregard his son's sound advice on how to improve profits because his son was a successful doctor and not a businessman.

Even children who love and respect their parents will routinely discount their parents' guidance on issues where they believe their parents aren't competent. I have a wonderful relationship with my teenage daughter. There's little we don't talk about. Philosophically, politically, and emotionally we're well matched and agree on most issues.

But I once tried to persuade her to enter the final phase of a horseback-riding competition even though she had been eliminated in an earlier phase. She absolutely refused. Even though I'd spent a lifetime competing in different sports, she knew I had no experience or knowledge of horseback riding. So my logic and reasoning had no influence on her. But when her twelve-year-old friend, who'd been riding since she was four, gave her the same advice, my daughter immediately agreed.

So, to be persuasive, it's not enough to be competent. People must perceive that you're competent in precisely the issues you're putting before them. And the hard fact is, sometimes that's just not possible. You may be smart, successful, and the world's leading recognized authority in whatever you do, but you just can't be competent at everything.

Fortunately, you don't have to be. You can still be persuasive in everyday life by teaming up with someone who is competent.

The best high-tech salesperson I've ever worked with knows almost nothing about technology, a shortcoming that's readily apparent to anyone who meets him. Yet throughout his career he has consistently been an outstanding producer.

Competence is not important in his case, because he makes it a point to partner with one or more technically competent colleagues as a selling team. The people he works with are always first-rate technicians who easily win Prospects' confidence. His Prospects see his selling team as competent and trustworthy, and he, as the team head, is persuasive.

This team approach to persuasion is particularly effective for professionals like lawyers, consultants, and engineers.

Prospects don't expect every professional to be an expert in every subject, but they nevertheless need to feel that the team they're hiring is competent. So senior partners and rainmakers in professional firms who are out of date with the latest developments in their professions, or who are unfamiliar with specialty areas, should always partner with specialists on client sales calls. Faking it is the kiss of death.

When the senior partner of a law firm that had done an assignment for my company called on me to propose helping us with some trademark issues, he brought with him the head of his firm's intellectual property group. Although I had the highest regard for the senior partner and his firm, he would not have won this additional business without the help of his partner. It made it possible for me to buy based on my perception of his firm's competence in intellectual property matters, not just on my trust in the senior partner.

This team selling approach is especially useful in high technology, where the firm's Poets—CEOs and other nontechnical officers—often call on prospects who are experts in their specialties and who expect, unreasonably, that the people calling on them will be equally expert. Worse still, many technologists are quick to brand nontechnical people as lower life forms—plankton on the technology food chain.

As a high-tech CEO, I would *never* make a call on a prospect or customer without someone from my company who was at least as technically knowledgeable as the smartest person the customer or prospect was bringing to the meeting. I made sure other executives followed the same rule. This way, my *company* was always perceived as technically competent, even if the executive on the call wasn't.

Overdelegating

Although teaming with a competent team member sounds like an easy way to solve a problem of low perceived competence, it doesn't always work. There are times when people expect you to be competent, and when delegating competence to someone else just isn't good enough.

If you're about to undergo a major operation, you want to know that the surgeon performing the procedure is competent. If you ask her questions about whatever malady you're suffering from, or about the operation she's planning to perform, and she keeps turning to her colleagues for answers, find a new doctor.

When Ronald Reagan was president, he surrounded himself with outstandingly competent advisers, men like Secretary of State George Shultz, Defense Secretary Casper Weinberger, Secretary of the Treasury Donald Regan, and chief of staff Jim Baker. Few people questioned the competence of Reagan's team, especially during his first term.

But the press and political analysts continually criticized Reagan for allowing himself to become detached from the issues and relying too much on his cabinet. While everyone understands that a president must turn to advisers for guidance, they nevertheless expect the president to become personally competent in issues of foreign and domestic policy. Not even the president of the United States can delegate competence when it comes to important leadership issues.

You may not be president of the United States, but there's a good chance people put the same demands on you. Your boss expects you to know what's going on in the department you manage. If it becomes apparent that you don't, and that you continually have to rely on people in your department to answer questions, your persuasiveness and your career are on shaky ground. If your client has hired you because she believes you're an expert in your field, and you continually turn to others for answers, there's a good chance she'll lose confidence in you, and you'll find it harder to get your way.

Even when you can delegate competence, it's still up to you to manage perceptions. You can't let your technical expert run your meetings. You can't let your valued assistant make independent proposals to your boss. When you delegate competence, you're saying that *your team* is competent and that your Prospect should be persuaded not necessarily by the individual to whom you've delegated competence, but by your team. As the team leader, that still leaves you with the responsibility to lead and manage conversations, and to be persuasive.

Gentle Persuasion Habit No. 9

Become competent. Know your stuff, do your homework, learn and demonstrate your competence. If you can't become an expert, team up with one.

13

Trustworthiness

IF HONESTY DID NOT EXIST, WE OUGHT TO INVENT
IT AS THE BEST MEANS OF GETTING RICH.

—Honoré de Mirabeau

If competence has a peer in persuasion, it's trustworthiness. Persuasion research has confirmed repeatedly that *trustworthiness and competence together are by far the most important personal characteristics affecting persuasiveness.* All else pales in comparison.

Unlike competence, which you may be able to assign to your team's designated expert, you can't delegate trustworthiness. People rely on your representations about your proposal's ability to meet their needs, its costs, and its value, compared with options they must forgo. If they doubt your trustworthiness, what you say won't give them the assurances they need so that the positive buying forces win out against the negative buying anxieties. But how do you create a perception of trustworthiness?

For decades I've watched people try to get others to believe in their trustworthiness. I've concluded that *people perceive only ordinary honest people and extraordinary con artists as trustworthy.* People are so sensitive to hypocrisy and deceit that ordinary people can't consistently fake trustworthiness. What follows is the four-part formula that works every time.

1. Be scrupulously and consistently honest in all your dealings. Consistency is critical, because people view trustworthiness as a defining character trait and not, like the way you dress, as something you can change to suit the circumstances.

What this means is that most people see you as either trustworthy or not. If you want people to believe you'll be honest with them, they must see that you're honest in your dealings with everyone, including your colleagues, superiors, subordinates, suppliers, family, and even your golf partners. If you deal dishonestly with one group and honestly with others, or are honest under some circumstances and dishonest under others, you won't be perceived as trustworthy.

For years a friend and I would occasionally play golf with a senior executive from a competing firm. He was an average golfer but a notorious cheat. In all the times I played with him, he never *recorded* a score above 77, but he never *played* below 90. I watched him hit five balls off the tee into the Arizona desert and still record a five for the hole instead of an honest fourteen. I never saw him hit a ball whose lie he didn't first improve, often by several yards.

Neither my friend nor I really knew the cheat's work performance, but neither of us would have been willing to give him a positive reference or hire him. We saw his meaningless cheating as evidence of a serious character flaw. It was hard for us to believe he was upstanding and honest in all the things in business that really mattered when he would be dishonest about something of no consequence.

2. Be fair. People associate fairness with trustworthiness. When you're unfair to someone financially, in your treatment of him, or in what you say about or to him, it's as if you stole something from him. Consequently, people who see you as unfair are less likely to see you as trustworthy.

When I was working for a Fortune 200 company, I had a woman executive in my department who was stealing from the company. This went on for nearly a year before I innocently questioned an expense, which led to an investigation. She was careful and clever, but the auditors caught her red-handed, falsifying expense reports, double-charging, trading in airline tickets, and submitting false receipts.

When the company discovered the theft, you could almost hear a collective gasp, with everyone who knew of the problem suddenly turning to me to see what I'd do, to see how justice would be served. Certainly no one was sympathetic to her plight; everyone felt she had let the team down and deserved whatever she got.

But my instinct told me to be fair—to be, in fact, far more than fair. Instead of firing her, I let her resign, but timed the resignation so she'd be paid a reasonable severance, even though she didn't deserve any severance whatsoever.

In a small meeting, I told the few people in my department who knew of the theft about the details of her severance, and gave strict instructions that no one was ever to say a negative word against the woman to anyone either inside or outside the company. People reacted with surprise and some outrage, feeling she deserved to be fired without severance and with a negative reference. My response was simply that we shouldn't make her life more difficult than she had just made it for herself. I ordered everyone to forget about the issue and move on with our business.

Several years later, when I was leaving the company, one of the people who had been in the meeting confided to me that the way I'd treated the woman had changed everything for him. Before the incident, he didn't know what to expect from me, and he always worried about his own job security. But he felt I'd been fair, and that was enough to make him trust me. He said that after the incident, he felt that if he did the best he could in his job, he'd be okay. He saw me as fair, and that was good enough for him.

Again, consistency is critical. You should be fair with everyone—subordinates, suppliers, family, and even competitors. (This doesn't mean you have to be nice to competitors, but only perceived as fair. There's more about how to treat competitors in chapter 21.)

3. Don't gossip or say negative things about others. If you say things about people that you wouldn't say to their faces, people perceive you as, if not dishonest, not entirely honest. So speaking poorly of others makes you appear less trustworthy, even if what you're saying is true.

An executive who worked for me took great pride in knowing everything about everyone. For a while everyone was eager to listen to his gossip about people in the industry, and he was only too happy to oblige, but this ended quickly. In a remarkably short time, no one trusted him and almost everyone actually came to dislike him.

If his gossip was positive, people saw it as boasting. If it was negative, they took his comments as hurtful and unfair. Even though people often enjoy listening to gossip, listening to this person talk about people who couldn't defend themselves seemed wrong, almost evil, and he lost his audience and support.

It wasn't that people believed that what he said about others was untrue, but they were concerned that he would betray personal trusts. People hesitated even to talk with the man for fear that he'd use what they said in negative gossip he'd pass along to others. Like the golf cheater's cheating, people saw his gossiping as evidence of a lack of trustworthiness. He became so unpopular and mistrusted within the company that in little more than a year I had to ask him to leave.

4. Don't tell people you're honest, fair, and trustworthy. Because no one, not even the most notorious cheat or liar, would claim differently, your claim won't be persuasive. It may even cause people to question your trustworthiness. As Ralph Waldo Emerson said, "The louder he talked of his honor, the faster we counted our spoons."

It's a simple formula: To be perceived as trustworthy, you must be trustworthy. Be scrupulously honest, fair, and positive, and the perceptions will take care of themselves *without your having to think much more about it.* This last phrase is important. The less you have to think about while you're working to get your way, the easier, more natural, and more effective you'll be.

Gentle Persuasion Habit No. 10

Be trustworthy. Be scrupulously and consistently honest, fair, and positive.

14

Other People's Interests

LET THE MOTIVE BE IN THE DEED AND NOT IN THE
EVENT. BE NOT ONE WHOSE MOTIVE FOR ACTION IS
THE HOPE OF REWARD.

—Krishna

You're involved in a perfectly normal conversation when the person you're talking to suddenly realizes you're trying to persuade him of something. Almost immediately, a pall falls over the conversation. Instinctively, unspoken questions form in the mind of the person you're trying to persuade: "Why are you trying to persuade me? What's in this for you? If I let you get your way, will I be tricked into doing something that's good for you but that may not be good for me?" And the most nagging question of all: "If I agree, will you win and will I lose?"

This fear of a hidden agenda is a powerful concern. Research shows that persuaders are generally not effective when the people they're trying to persuade believe the persuader has a vested interest in the outcome. This is no small thing, and if it's important that you get your way, you ignore it at your peril. But before we can develop a strategy for dealing with this persuasion dynamic, we must accept two key facts.

The first is that what people are most worried about, that

you have a vested interest in the outcome, is true. Hey, you're no different from anyone else. You're motivated by your own personal needs, and if there weren't something in it for you, something that meets one or more of your own personal needs, you wouldn't be spending your time and energy trying to get your way.

The second fact you must accept is that it's hopeless to try to deny or hide that you have something to gain. People aren't easily fooled; if you deny your interests, you won't be believed.

This puts you in a tough situation. If you admit your self-interest, your arguments will be suspect and less persuasive. If you deny it, you won't be believed and you won't appear trustworthy. Either way, it seems as if your persuasiveness takes a hit.

Fortunately, there's a solution to this dilemma. You must align your personal needs with your Prospects' personal needs, and make your Prospects understand that you can fulfill your needs only if you fulfill theirs first. In other words, you win only if your Prospects win. If you do this, your Prospect won't hold it against you that you also have something to gain. On the contrary, that you both have something to gain will make you more persuasive. Persuasiveness research shows that, all other things being equal, people are more likely to agree with you if you share common goals.

How does this work in practice? If you provide any kind of service, from investment banking to house cleaning, and refuse to accept payment unless your Prospect agrees his needs have been fulfilled, you've aligned your needs with your Prospect's. For example, if you're a lawyer working on contingency, it's easier for your clients to believe you share the same objectives.

The most successful relationships in families happen when the parents' goals are aligned with their children's and the worst when they're not. The Williams family were my neighbors when I was growing up. Like most fathers, Mr. Williams wanted his two daughters to grow up to be successful, and he believed academic achievement was the key to success.

Because raising successful children is a compelling need, and because children's accomplishments and success give their parents status and recognition among their friends and relatives, Mr. Williams had a need for his children to do well in school. Besides declaring his expectations in no uncertain terms, he did not take any special steps to help his children develop any compelling need of their own that could be fulfilled through academic achievement.

So chance prevailed. The older daughter, Elizabeth, through some mysterious confluence of forces, developed a love of learning and school. Her younger sister, Carol, developed a love of sports, which her father neither understood nor respected.

I was too young to appreciate it at the time, but this was a perfect example of the effect of goal alignment. Mr. Williams and Elizabeth had a wonderful relationship, free of tension. With her, Mr. Williams easily got his way on things that mattered.

But his relationship with Carol, who was as intelligent and driven as Elizabeth, was World War III. Mr. Williams refused to support Carol's athletic aspirations either emotionally or financially. In his value system, sports were a waste of time and energy.

Both Elizabeth and Carol eventually became successful, but Mr. Williams's relationship with Carol was tension-filled, vituperative, and sad, and stayed that way for his entire life. Although he was a good father who claimed, and believed, to be driven only by his children's needs, Carol wasn't fooled. She understood instinctively that her father's needs were not aligned with hers. He had no influence over her except by invoking his parental authority, and even this disappeared before she reached her teens.

What Mr. Williams should have done was listen to Carol and understand her needs. Although I did not see it at the time, Elizabeth had won recognition through her accomplishments, and, as is common among siblings, Carol needed equal recognition. But equal recognition solely through academic achievement was nearly impossible for Carol, given Elizabeth's outstanding performance in the same school system, the same subjects, and even the same teachers.

If Mr. Williams would have understood Carol's need for recognition, he could have supported and encouraged Carol's athletic achievements while at the same time praising her academic accomplishments, even if they were not quite as outstanding as her sister's. Instead he continually disparaged Carol's performance at school by comparing it with Elizabeth's. So academic achievements brought Carol no recognition whatsoever with her family.

But, even worse, by not supporting Carol's athletic aspirations with lessons, coaching, and moral support, it seemed to Carol that he was fighting her effort to fulfill her needs. It's little wonder that father and daughter never reconciled. While working to fulfill his own needs, he worked to ensure that Carol couldn't fulfill her own. Instead of trying to change Carol's needs, he should have figured out how to fulfill his own by fulfilling hers.

Harry Truman showed great insight when he said, "I found the best way to give advice to your children is to find out what they want and then advise them to do it." Then not only will they do what you ask, but you can also maintain a loving, functional relationship.

Like Mr. Williams and Elizabeth, when your goals are aligned with your Prospects', when your Prospects understand that you can fulfill your own needs only if you first fulfill theirs, suspicion and distrust will melt away, and your words will be persuasive. You'll be on automatic pilot to getting your way.

Gentle Persuasion Habit No. 11

Put the personal needs of others first, and then align your needs with theirs.

15

Personal Packaging

WE FIND FOR THE DEFENDANT, MUCH AS WE
DISLIKE HIM.

—*A. P. Herbert*

Competence, trustworthiness, and putting other people's interests first moves you a long way toward getting your way in everyday life. But there's still some fine-tuning you can do, some packaging of yourself that can help you be more persuasive. This personal packaging is most useful when what you're selling is unimportant to your Prospect, but it never hurts to get everything right no matter what you're selling.

The personal characteristics we'll discuss in this chapter are first impressions, appearance, dress, body language, handshake, personal trademarks, being liked, and your similarity to your Prospect. These are included here not because they're such important factors in getting your way, but because too many people mistakenly think they are. We're discussing them for perspective, not for emphasis.

First Impressions

The psychology underlying first impressions is scary. Within seconds of meeting you, people begin to form their opinions and beliefs about you. Then, if those initial beliefs are strongly positive or negative, these people you've just met, who really know nothing about you, filter and sort new information so that it's consistent with their initial impressions. It's possible that what they believe about you after just four minutes can be so set that you'll have a tough time changing their minds.

If you came to your first meeting with a prospective client with a little piece of toilet paper still stuck to that razor nick on your chin, and you crushed her hand with a gorilla handshake, she's going to pay special attention to, and believe, negative information about you that confirms the strong negative first impression you made.

To make matters worse, in a perverse quirk of human nature, people naturally pay more attention to, and are more likely to believe, negative information. As a result, *strongly negative first impressions are especially enduring.* So if she thinks you're a jerk three seconds after meeting you, there's a good chance the rest of your meeting is headed deep into jerk territory.

Nevertheless, contrary to popular opinion, people's beliefs and attitudes toward you are not necessarily *unalterably* set by first impressions. If the first impression you made wasn't strongly positive or negative, people will objectively listen to and think about later information. If your proposal is important to your Prospect, she'll focus on the logic and supporting story of your proposal and less on you, even if you made a strong first impression. If you're a lawyer who can recover $100 million for the prospective client you've just met, and if you appear competent and trustworthy and make a credible case during the meeting, she may be willing to overlook the razor nick and the bruiser handshake.

Still, if you make a really poor first impression, you've needlessly set yourself facing an uphill battle that's tough to win. On the other hand, you're not going to sign up a million-dollar new client or be made CEO as a result of a great first impression based on your handshake or the cut of your suit. Instead of saying, "You never get a second chance to make a good first impression," a more useful thought would be "You never get a second chance not to make a bad first impression."

This takes some of the pressure off you before your first meeting with a Prospect. If your proposal is important to your Prospect, your objective should be to get through the initial four minutes or so with a neutral to slightly positive impression. This prepares people to listen to what you have to say with an open or even a positive mind. That's what you really want to accomplish with a first impression, not to make the actual sale.

Appearance

Fortunately for the average Poet, appearance matters most when people are making decisions that are unimportant to them. When something is important, Prospects look past looks, and are most influenced by their perception of the logic and facts.

That's bad if you aspire to be a spokesperson for athletic shoes, vitamins, or aftershave, but in the major issues in life, your competence, trustworthiness, and persuasive skills will pull you through just fine. Nevertheless, most people worry about their appearance, about how attractive they are. As it turns out, up to a point it's worth the worry.

Research confirms that, unfair as it may be, attractive people are more persuasive than unattractive people. But it's my experience that this effect works only at the extremes of attractiveness. In the great middle, where most people fall, the playing field is pretty level. Sure, only the prettiest girls in the school have a crack at being homecoming queen, and Quasimodo will never have a sneaker named after him, but you don't have to be Robert Redford or Sharon Stone to land the biggest jobs or win the best clients. The average CEO is no more attractive than the average Joe or Jane. Some are downright unattractive.

The bottom line here is that attractiveness is just not that important for us ordinary Poets. While there's a God-given natural limit to how handsome or beautiful someone can be, everyone is attractive enough to manage his or her overall appearance to fall into at least the middle range. All it takes is careful grooming, dress, and style to make yourself as attractive as you can be.

Dress

At one time this issue was clear—the way you dressed mattered. Researchers even identified specific outfits that were most effective for gaining respect and getting your way in business.

But then along came "casual Friday," followed by casual every day of the week. The effect of this nearly overnight social transformation has been to leave too many people believing that "casual dress" means "it doesn't matter what you wear as long as you're not arrested." Suddenly, people earning, or hoping eventually to earn, six-figure incomes show up at the office dressed as if they work at the car wash.

Don't be fooled. While organizations may *tolerate* all sorts and manner of casual dress, what you wear still influences people's impressions of you and how persuasive you are. Having the option or, in many companies, the requirement to dress casually doesn't mean you can throw on your cleanest dirty T-shirt and a pair of beat-up jeans and Nikes and still be taken seriously, *even if you're the all-time Whiz of the Western World in your field.*

This book is not the forum to review all the nuances of traditional and casual dress. *Dress Casually for Success . . . For*

Men, by Mark Weber; Simple Chic's *Work Clothes; Casual Dress for Serious Work,* by Kim Gross and Jeff Stone; and *New Dress for Success* and *New Woman's Dress for Success,* both by John T. Molloy, are all excellent. Read them and follow their advice. If you want to get your way in everyday life, they'll make a difference.

To make your fashion decisions easier, here are two simple rules:

•Dress in a way that doesn't create inconsistencies between your message and your appearance. If you're a serious accountant responsible for serious accounting stuff, don't come to work—or, worse, to a job interview—dressed like a chimney sweep, even if that's the way the CEO dresses. On the other hand, if your message is that you're a creative genius, don't dress like a serious accountant. When people sense even minor inconsistencies between your appearance and the message you're trying to deliver, they become uneasy and distracted, even suspicious. This makes persuasion difficult if not impossible.

•In business and professional settings, dress about as casually or as formally as your Prospects dress. Of course, your dress must be consistent with the message you're delivering, but too big a difference in the way you dress compared with the people around you draws attention to clothes and causes everyone to be uncomfortable.

Just as a lawyer calling on a sandals-and-T-shirt-wearing Silicon Valley CEO shouldn't show up in sandals and a T-shirt (it's inconsistent with the lawyer's message), neither would it be effective to make the call decked out in a white shirt, a $2,000 double-breasted suit, a Hermès tie, and three points of his handkerchief rising out of his jacket's breast pocket like snow-covered mountain peaks glistening on the horizon; it's too different from his "surroundings." Neither costume—and what you wear is a costume designed to support a role—is likely to help him persuade his Prospect.

I never fully appreciated the importance of these two rules on persuasion until I had an enlightening experience while I was running a software company. An important Danish Prospect had come to the United States to visit with my company and with all our competitors. Traveling with a team of six technical people, his purpose was to evaluate all the available products and vendors and recommend the best product for use by a large group of Danish government agencies.

Because of the group's travel schedule, the meeting with my company was scheduled at our New York City offices, with my chief technology officer and I leading the meeting. One question was, "What do we wear?"

Our worry was that if we showed up in suits and ties and the Prospect dressed casually, or if we dressed casually and the Prospect wore suits and ties, the difference in the way the two groups dressed would make our guests feel uncomfortable. Also, it might send the wrong message. If we dressed casually, the Prospect might feel we weren't showing them adequate respect or taking them seriously; but if we dressed in suits and ties, we might not look like the high-tech company we were.

We decided not to guess. The salesperson on the account called our Prospect and suggested everyone come dressed casually. They readily agreed. The salesperson even helped define what he meant by casual, by warning them that most people in the company wore jeans.

On the day of the meeting, the Prospect's people were the most casually dressed, most in sweatshirts and running shoes. When the Danish project leader saw that the chief technology officer and I also wore jeans, his first comment, even before we were introduced, was, "Even the CEO wears jeans. Now this is what I expect of an American high-tech company."

The meeting, which was the first on the Prospect's tour, was a success, we eventually won the account, and the project leader became a customer and friend. He later confided that it stood out in his mind that the company's two top officers would come to a meeting with a Prospect in Manhattan wearing jeans. It set the right tone and was in sharp contrast to our competition, all of whom worked for divisions of large, conservative companies and all of whom wore suits and ties. He felt as if his other meetings were with bankers or accountants and not with real high-tech companies.

Of course, we didn't win the account based just on clothes. But the way we dressed was consistent with our message of being a high-tech, creative company. Because everyone dressed similarly, everyone was comfortable. Although clothes didn't make the sale, they opened the communications channels and helped make us more persuasive.

Think of yourself as a playwright and of the way you dress as your character's costume. Spend no more (or less) time or energy worrying about your clothes than a playwright does worrying about her actors' costumes. Dress appropriately for your role and the scene, and everyone will feel comfortable and be able to concentrate on your message.

Body Language

Over half the information people use to form their opinions of you comes not from what you say, but from body language—your posture, facial expressions, gestures, eye contact, how close you stand to people, and the way you sit, stand, and walk.

Researchers have cataloged a detailed inventory of body language and people's interpretations of it. But the important question is whether this research can help you manage your nonverbal communications in everyday life. Get ready for a shocker, because my conclusion is that it can't. As a certified Poet, you shouldn't try to manage your body language. Act naturally, go with the flow, and if you're competent and trustworthy and put other people's interests first, you'll do just fine.

Several practical considerations lead to this advice. The first is that trying to manage your body language while simultaneously having an intelligent conversation and being hyperalert for what people are saying about their personal needs and buying anxieties is *really* hard work. You'll waste your attention and energy focusing on dozens of nearly insignificant personal gestures and postures that should be natural and require no energy or attention. You'll be thinking about yourself instead of about your Prospect, the exact opposite of what you need to do to be persuasive.

But more important than having to divert your energy and attention from others to yourself is the question of whether normal people can believably use body language to communicate something they don't feel or believe. That is, whether they can be believable nonverbal liars.

Of course, some people can, just as some people can be credible oral liars. But most people can't. Even if you're smiling, maintaining eye contact, sitting up straight, keeping your hands away from your face, leaning toward your listener, and generally doing everything recommended to convey confidence, trustworthiness, and power, if that's not you, you can be sure it's not coming off.

Managing your body language is not the secret to getting your way. The only sure strategy is to sincerely embrace the three core values of competence, trustworthiness, and putting other people's interests first. When you know your stuff inside out, and when you believe in what you're selling and its value to others, your body language will broadcast your sincerity without your having to think about it.

Shake

A fiftyish professional woman, a CPA with a law degree, recently visited our offices. When she shook my hand, it felt as if she'd handed me a veal cutlet that had been left out of the refrigerator too long. Even though I know better than to be influenced by a personal characteristic as insignificant as a handshake, she made a poor first impression.

Shaking hands isn't rocket science. Most people have it right before they leave their teens. Grasp the other person's entire hand, squeeze with a firm but not overpowering grip, *look the person straight in the eyes*, say sincerely that you're delighted to meet her or see her again, shake for two or three seconds, and it's done.

The only other question is when to shake hands and with whom, and again the answer is simple. In Western settings (and generally in economically developed Eastern ones also), always offer your hand to everyone—man, woman, or child, boss, subordinate, or peer. It doesn't matter whether you're a custodian or a CEO, or whether the person you're meeting is a field hand or a diplomat, and it doesn't matter how old or what gender you are.

It's a gesture that today says, "Hello, I'm delighted to meet you," or "Good-bye, I really enjoyed meeting you." If that's what's really in your mind and heart, you'll never go wrong—you'll never make a bad impression—by offering to shake hands. Ignore any advice that tells you differently, such as that young people or women shouldn't initiate shaking hands. It's hogwash.

Personal Trademarks

Personal trademarks are characteristics that set you apart from others. They can range from beards to men's ponytails, from big ears to bow ties, from being overweight to being over-cologned, from formal dress in casual settings to casual dress in formal settings, from commuting by bicycle to commuting by limo, from unusual hobbies to unusual accomplishments. Motorcycling and ballooning were trademarks of the late Malcolm Forbes; big ears are Ross Perot's.

The above-mentioned personal trademarks have one thing in common: In selling and persuasion situations, they're distractions that draw attention away from your message and draw it to you. This can either work to your advantage or against it.

If you're already perceived as credible and trustworthy, a personal trademark will call more attention to you, which should be helpful. If you haven't established your competence and trustworthiness, personal trademarks can work against you by distracting people from your message. It makes sense, then, to avoid trademarks if you haven't yet established a strong personal reputation. If you really have to wear a handlebar mustache or dye your hair orange, do it after you're famous, not before the interviews for your first job.

In any case, if you adopt a personal trademark, be sure it doesn't undermine your perceived competence and trustworthiness. A short, well-trimmed beard worn by a lawyer with an established reputation would be neutral. If you show up looking like ZZ Top, however, your judgment will be open to question, and the personal trademark will be negative.

Best of all is a positive trademark that reinforces the perception of competence and trustworthiness. Mountain climbing or competing in triathlons can be a positive trademark if high energy, competitiveness, endurance, and tenacity are part of your competence profile.

Oh, to Be Liked

Selling is a land fertile with folklore and conventional wisdom, but the most widely believed idea is that *people buy from people they like.* Nearly all sales training material espouses this "fact" of selling and bases essential advice on it.

This proclamation is, if not false, at least content-free. For a start, people often buy from people they don't like, but whose offering meets their needs. My friend Chuck, the CEO of a local company, bought software critical to his day-to-day business from a salesperson he truly disliked. He bought it in spite of the salesman, because it's the best software for his needs, at the best price.

Not only will people buy from people they don't like, but they often don't buy from people they do like. If I like a salesman, but his product or service doesn't meet my needs, no sale.

Finally, it's also true that people won't buy from people they don't like, just as it's true they'll buy from people they do like. So we've got all the bases covered. People buy from people they like, they don't buy from people they like, they buy from people they don't like, and they don't buy from people they don't like. It all depends. And what it all depends on is whether the seller can meet the buyer's collage of needs.

What sales pundits really mean when they say people buy from people they like is that, *all other things being equal, people buy from people they like.* In other words, it's better to be liked than not liked, an idea it's hard to argue with. Whether you're a salesperson, a lawyer, a kindergarten teacher, or a bus driver, you're certainly more likely to succeed, all other things being equal, if you're liked than if you're not liked.

Psychological research confirms that people are more likely to agree with people they like. But this holds true primarily for unimportant issues that people don't take the time to think about. If the issues are important enough to think about, the underlying logic and evidence still win the day.

So once again Poets everywhere can breathe a sigh of relief. You don't have to spend time and energy trying to be liked—which is a good thing because, paradoxically, people often dislike people who try too hard to be liked. It's one of the reasons so many people don't like salespeople, and one of the reasons Poets dread selling. Poets think they somehow have to get everyone to like them, when what they really want to do is go out there and be truly great at whatever they do.

Forget about working to be liked. Know your stuff, be trustworthy, and put other people's interests first. If the issues are important to your Prospect, you'll be liked as much as you need to be.

Similarity

Early psychology research and conventional wisdom conclude that if you want to persuade people you should appear to be as similar to them as possible. So politicians who went to Exeter and Yale and were raised with servants and trust funds don red flannel shirts and goofy hats to establish their kinship with Joe Voter.

But further thought, and later research, shows that it's not as simple as that. Similarity to the person you're trying to persuade can help you, have no effect, or hurt you.

Perceived similarity to your Prospect will increase your persuasiveness if it increases your perceived competence and trustworthiness. If you both belong to the same church, your Prospect may believe you're more likely to be trustworthy. If you're selling professional services to programmers and you have a computer science background, your persuasiveness may increase because your Prospects view you as more competent.

But if the similarities are on irrelevant points that don't reflect on your competence or trustworthiness, they may not matter. That you and your Prospect both play golf or root for the Yankees may help you keep a conversation going, but it won't help you sell nuclear reactors if your Prospect doesn't think you're competent.

In some situations, being different from your Prospect may increase your persuasiveness. If you dressed, spoke, and acted like your children, you'd be less persuasive with them in most parental matters. Despite their protestations to the contrary, children need to see their parents as different from them— more knowledgeable and experienced, older and wiser.

If you dropped out of high school and now work as an hourly laborer, you'll be more persuaded by well-educated, well-dressed professionals than by your cousin Bubba who's your spitting image. Certainly you're not going to take medical advice from Bubba over a doctor's on your heart condition, or let Bubba instead of a lawyer represent you in court. To some extent, it's the difference between you and the professionals that makes the professionals more persuasive.

The value of perceived similarities or differences is to help you appear more competent and trustworthy. It makes sense for union leaders to be seen as similar to their union rank and file, and for doctors to wear white coats and look different from their patients. So worry about your message, not about finding meaningless similarities with your Prospect.

Family Matters

The advice in this chapter is most relevant to persuasion in your business or professional life, where people who don't know you as well as your friends and family do form their perceptions based on superficial characteristics. But is it relevant to your family or personal life? Almost certainly.

In all aspects of your everyday life, whether personal or commercial, if you're perceived as competent and trustworthy and as someone who always puts others' needs first, none of the characteristics this chapter deals with counts for much. You're going to be happy, successful, and persuasive. It won't matter if you dress like a slob at home or, like my friend Roger, wear a sports jacket and penny loafers to rake the leaves.

But one word of warning: Be careful if your habits with family and friends are very different from your habits in your business or professional life. If you dress to the nines for work and are a slob at home, you may be signaling indifference to your family's opinions of you. Or that you're trying to be something at work you really aren't. Or that you take your family for granted.

This isn't to say you have to start dressing for dinner at home, but wild inconsistencies make people uncomfortable and often lead to questions about your general trustworthiness. My advice is to dress, act, and speak in the same way with your friends and family as you would in similar circumstances with people from your business or professional life. No one, not even the people closest to you, likes to be taken for granted.

Gentle Persuasion Habits Nos. 12 and 13

- *Don't worry about body language, being liked, being similar to others, or making an outstanding first impression. If you're competent, trustworthy, and put other people's interests first, just be yourself.*
- *Key the way you dress to the way others dress, but always dress in a way that's consistent with your message.*

Step 3

Communicate Persuasively

16

What We Have Here Is a Failure to Communicate

THE WORLD IS DIVIDED INTO TWO TYPES OF PEOPLE:
THOSE WHO LOVE TO TALK, AND THOSE WHO HATE
TO LISTEN.

—*James Thorpe*

Why all the fuss? "After all," Poets typically think, "if I'm competent, trustworthy, and can genuinely help people, it should be enough for me to describe honestly and clearly what I have to offer." But the problem is, even though you think you're getting through, much of the time you're Talking Without Communicating.

One summer afternoon I passed Doug's office as he was interviewing Ben, an applicant for a senior position in our company. As in most interviews, the applicant was doing the talking, and the interviewer was smiling and nodding.

I interviewed Ben next, and asked how his previous meeting had gone. His response was, "Great. Doug's a great guy. We had a great conversation. Great."

After my interview, I asked Doug what he thought of Ben. His response was, "I'm not really sure. I went for a run during lunchtime, my office was too warm, and I was so tired I had to drive my fingernails into the palm of my hand to keep from falling asleep."

Here was a job seeker who traveled seven hundred miles for an important interview, who really wanted the job, and who thought he was communicating. But the person he was talking to (certainly not communicating with) was only thinking about not falling out of his chair and embarrassing himself. Ben was Talking Without Communicating.

Maybe you think this is an unusual case because of Doug's run. But it's not, because the run wasn't the problem. If Ben had been talking about something Doug was interested in— say, how Doug could cut fifteen minutes off his marathon time or retire in luxury in two years—Doug would have been fully awake and processing information like a Cray supercomputer. He would have heard and remembered everything despite his run and the warm office. The real problem was that people are "me-centered"—their interests center around their own needs—and Ben was talking about himself and not about Doug.

That people's attention is centered on *their* needs is unfortunate for you if you want people to pay attention to *your* needs. In one form or another, you're saying, "Look here, listen to me, think about what I'm saying." But deep in the other guy's brain, he's thinking, "I'm going to fall asleep in front of this guy and look like a moron," or "I shouldn't have had that second doughnut," or "I think I forgot to clean the cat box," or "How is this person trying to fool me?" or just about anything completely irrelevant to whatever you want the other person to pay attention to.

This is happening even if your Prospect is looking at you and seems to be paying attention. Sure, she's listening, but only in the sense that sound waves from your voice vibrate her eardrums. Your words are not registering in her brain *the specific message you want to communicate*. That's what Talking Without Communicating is—vibrating people's eardrums without delivering the message you intend to their brains.

You may say, "I'd like to meet with you to discuss something I think you'll find useful," or "Customer satisfaction is our most important product," or "We take pride in our reputation for integrity," or "We have the best people in the industry." If you're interviewing for a job, you say, "I am a hard worker and a fast learner," or if you're talking to your daughter, "I'm your mother and I'm doing this for your own good."

You may believe what you're saying with all your heart, and what you're saying may be 100-percent true, but for the most part, statements like these have absolutely zero communication value. They're you talking about yourself, your practice, your proposal, about what you want or believe, or about your products. They're not about what your Prospect is interested in—which is himself. If you could take a snapshot of your listener's brain when your "me-centered" message hits it, you'd see a screen saver.

Too Much Noise

Talking to me-centered Prospects is just one small part of your communications challenge. To understand what you're up against, try this simple experiment:

Think back to the last time you watched TV or listened to the radio. Probably it wasn't that long ago; maybe you watched TV yesterday evening or listened to the radio in the car on the on the way home from work or the store. Take a pencil and paper and write down a list of the advertisers and the message each was trying to communicate. Beside each message, write down what you did differently because of what you heard or saw.

Don't feel bad if you find yourself staring at a blank sheet of paper. In one study of 13,000 people, 93 percent couldn't recall even the most recent advertisement they were exposed to—so forget about remembering or being persuaded by the ads' messages.

Most messages aren't received; if they're received, they're

not remembered; if they're remembered, they're not believed; even if they're believed, they don't persuade people to act. But if a message isn't heard, believed, remembered, and acted on, it's just content-free words, not effective communication.

Unfortunately this content-free bombardment—whether in résumés, e-mails, reports, or proposals, or in newspapers, magazines, television, radio, direct mail, or billboards—affects *your* ability to communicate effectively. There's a cacophony of messages overwhelming the people you're trying to get to. It makes effective communication difficult even if you're a Poet with a unique and valuable idea or proposal.

Too bad for us Poets, but the communication airways are crammed with signals that jam our messages. People's attention is hopelessly fragmented, and their minds are dulled to what you're saying, dulled by a thousand messages a day, 365 days a year, every year of their lives. Even when you're talking about your Prospect and it's to her benefit to listen to and remember what you're saying, your message has to compete with thousands of other messages for her limited attention, processing time, and memory.

To be noticed, understood, and believed, you must do something different. But since everyone is trying to do something different, you must do something different from what everyone else is trying to do. If this all sounds crazy and impossible, you're beginning to appreciate the communication challenge.

Don't be discouraged. What you must do differently is not talk more, but *think* more. This surprises people, because they think of persuasion, of getting your way, as *talking people into doing what you want*. It isn't. It's precise, disciplined communication, and talking is only a small part of the process. When it comes to getting your way in everyday life, talking is to persuasion as typing is to writing.

Persuading people will be far easier and more pleasant if you develop a focused communication strategy. You won't have to talk as much. When you're really cooking, people will have a vivid mental picture of who you are and why they should listen to you. They'll be predisposed to accept you, your ideas, and your services. Life will be good.

Gentle Persuasion Habit No. 14

Talk to people in terms of their interests and needs, not in terms of your interests and needs.

When we talk about persuasion in the rest of this book, it will usually be in the context of a "meeting," during which you make a "presentation," even if the meeting is an informal conversation. You may be calling on a client to sell him your services, or talking to your boss over a beer after a round of golf, to peers during a casual lunch, or with your teenage son as you drive to the mall.

Whatever the venue, you're "meeting" with your Prospect. You've taken the time to learn about her personal needs, and you're ready to present your proposal. The first thing to do is to get her attention. Don't assume you've got it just because only the two of you are in the room, and she's looking at you and seems to be listening. Her mind may be miles away, and what you're about to say is no more than an upcoming speed bump on her mental journey to somewhere else.

17

Attention Kmart Shoppers!

WHO WOULD SUCCEED IN THE WORLD SHOULD BE
WISE IN THE USE OF HIS PRONOUNS. UTTER THE YOU
TWENTY TIMES, WHERE YOU ONCE UTTER THE I.

—*John Milton Hay*

You're home watching TV. The program ends, and a commercial comes on. It doesn't sell you anything because you're not listening to it. Your mind, even if not accompanied by your actual body, has left the room.

Suddenly an emergency weather broadcast scrolls across the bottom of the screen, preceded by a loud, intermittent beeping that draws your attention to the coming message. The first words of the broadcast tell you that the message is a "severe weather warning" for your county. Now you're fully engaged, paying attention to the message and ready to process information.

This is the model you should follow when you begin to discuss a topic that's important to you. Get your listeners' attention and interest them enough to think about what you're going to say.

If you don't, you'll be Talking Without Communicating.

Because most people aren't rude or unkind, they won't just turn their backs on you and walk away, leaving you feeling foolish and certain you made no impression on them. Instead, they'll look at you, nod occasionally, and let you talk until you're done, or at least until they can find a socially acceptable way to escape. They'll even respond politely as you talk. As a result, you'll leave the conversation thinking you actually communicated and accomplished something. Other than vibrating their eardrums, you did not.

You, You, You

Before you can be persuasive, you must get your listeners' attention and motivate them to listen to what you're about to say. Fortunately, there's a simple and effective way to gain attention in ordinary conversation. It starts with two words people always respond to—their names and the word *you*.

"*John*, I'm going to tell *you* a story *you'll* find interesting. It relates directly to *your* career in the company."

This kind of opening statement acts like the emergency weather broadcast. It says, "Pay attention because we're going to talk about you, or about something you'll find important, interesting, or useful." Contrast this with an opening that begins, "If you don't mind, I'd like to take a few minutes and tell you about my services." This is you talking about yourself, and the words *me* and *I* are definitely not interesting to most people.

But just using the word *you* is not enough. It's like the joke about the self-absorbed actor who, after thirty minutes of talking about himself, says, "But that's enough about me. Let's talk about you now. What do you think about me?"

That's not very different from saying, "If *you* don't mind, *I'd* like to take a few minutes and tell *you* about *my* services." Or, if you're a parent and you say to your child, "We need to talk about your grades," you're really saying that *you* want to talk about *your* opinions and *your* concerns and what's on *your* mind. For the word *you* to capture attention, the listener has to believe that what's about to be said is really going to be about her.

Stories and Mystery

Another way to get your listener's attention is to mix in one or two more ingredients. First, people will always listen intently to interesting, relevant stories, but will usually tune out lectures, sermons, and fact recitations. Second, it's effective to introduce an element of mystery, an announcement that there's something unknown coming that you'll clear up.

You're interviewing for a job and meeting with the head of human resources. "Filling this job must be an interesting challenge for *you*. I can see where *you'd* have to make some difficult trade-offs to find someone with the experience to please everyone *you* answer to on the search. I'd like to tell *you* about what happened at my last job and maybe *you* can tell me if I fit the profile *you're* looking for."

Contrast this with, "Maybe I should start by summarizing my experience." The first approach relates what you're about to say to the listener's needs and interests, introduces an element of mystery (will my experience be relevant?), and tells the interviewer you're about to tell a story. The second opening prepares the listener for a recitation of facts.

If you're a professional calling on a prospective client, you might begin, "One of our clients is facing the same problem *you're* facing. I think *you'll* be interested to hear how they dealt with the same issues *you* have." Contrast this with, "Let me tell you about our firm."

You're about to talk to your teenager about his driving habits, so you begin, "There's an article in the paper about new drivers like *you*. I think *you'll* find it interesting." This is far more likely to capture your child's attention than "I want to talk about your driving habits," which is equivalent to an emergency broadcast that says, "Warning, lecture approaching, head for the hills."

Old-Fogeyism

Just a word of warning. While people love to listen to good stories, it's important that the stories be interesting and relevant *to the listener.* Parents who tell their children how they walked ten miles to school every day in rain and snow, uphill both ways, are not telling an interesting story their children can relate to. They're acting like old fogeys.

This may sound silly, but it happens too often in everyday life. A senior partner trying to make a point with a client or a new associate tells stories from his past. If the stories are meant to highlight the partner's brilliance and wit rather than make a relevant point, or if the listeners can't relate to the story because of time, place, or circumstances, they mentally roll their eyes and classify the speaker as an old fogey.

On the other hand, I worked for a CEO who had a story for every occasion. They were always to the point, funny, and interesting, often highlighting mistakes he'd made in the past. They were so effective that employees retold them for years. Indeed, I still tell his stories, twenty-five years later. No old-fogeyism here, even though he was decades older than most of his employees. The stories kept people's attention and made him more persuasive.

It doesn't take much. Before talking, you must say something that captures your listener's attention, an emergency weather broadcast announcement that says that what's coming will be interesting and relevant, so pay attention. Use people's names and the pronoun *you,* tell your listeners you're going to talk about something relevant to them, let them know you're going to tell an interesting story, and include an element of mystery. Then people will pay attention and think about what you say.

Gentle Persuasion Habit No. 15

Get people's attention before you talk.

18

Personal Positioning

PUT IT BEFORE THEM BRIEFLY SO THEY WILL READ IT,
CLEARLY SO THEY WILL APPRECIATE IT,
PICTURESQUELY SO THEY WILL REMEMBER IT AND,
ABOVE ALL, ACCURATELY SO THEY WILL BE GUIDED
BY ITS LIGHT.

—*Joseph Pulitzer*

Cars are amazingly complex things, the result of thousands of engineering decisions that produce hundreds of different makes and models, each with unique handling, performance, safety features, and purchase and maintenance costs. Who cares?

When it's time to buy a new one, you don't study specifications and performance data. You don't even look at all the different makes and models, visiting Chrysler, Rolls-Royce, Porsche, Hyundai, Lexus, Chevrolet, and Volvo dealers to compare products. These cars all convey such different mental images that if you're interested in one, you're probably not interested in the others.

You make your selection based on what you already know about cars. It doesn't matter that, if you're like most people, you don't know much. Millions of intelligent people make the second-largest purchase in their lives based on strong opinions about something they really know little about.

If you've developed opinions about cars—say, that Volvos are safe, BMWs fun to drive, Mercedes well engineered, and Chevrolets economical to own—it's in large part because car companies began selling to you long before you were in the market for a car. They created beliefs and biases about their products in your mind through what's known in marketing as "positioning." *Positioning is the process of establishing a vivid picture in people's minds of what products stand for and how they fulfill different needs.*

Product positioning is something companies do primarily to the minds of their prospects and buyers, and only secondarily something they do to the products themselves. That Pepsi is a drink for the younger generation has nothing to do with Pepsi as a product. It has to do with the way the company positions the product in buyers' minds. Marlboros and Virginia Slims are fundamentally the same product. It's the way they're positioned that makes them appeal to different types of buyers.*

Once a product owns a position in your mind, meaning you've developed strong beliefs about what it is and what it stands for, this position acts as the lens through which you view the product and new information about it. You'll believe that Volvos are safer than GM products, that German cars are better engineered than British cars, and that thirty-year-old VW Beetles are more durable than modern Fords. It will take a preponderance of evidence to change your views, and sometimes not even that will do it. The car companies have used positioning to persuade you to believe what they want you to believe.

Like products, individuals have positions in people's minds. Your personal position, that is, who people *think* you are, how competent and trustworthy they *think* you are, and what they *think* you do, has an enormous influence on your persuasive-

---

*That said, the product itself does affect positioning options. Poli-Grip can't be positioned as the denture adhesive of the younger generation, nor Red Man as the supermodels' chewing tobacco.

ness. It affects the way people interpret facts about you and about your ideas and proposals. It's the lens though which people view you.

If you're positioned in your clients' minds as a brilliant accountant, they're more likely to see your error on their tax return as an unusual oversight than if you're positioned in their minds as a rookie. If you're positioned as a successful artist, your painting will probably gain more respect than an identical work signed by an unknown.

To the extent that you can control this mental picture—that you can make it vivid, sharp, and distinctive—you influence people's responses to you and to your requests. You control how easy it is to get your way in everyday life. And like product position, your personal position is determined at least as much by what you do to people's minds as what you do to yourself.

Macro-Positioning

Positioning is so important in selling that marketing departments staffed with specialists devote multimillion-dollar advertising and public relations budgets to creating unique positions for products and the companies that sell them. You, on the other hand, are on your own. How can a single person do what legions of advertising and marketing people are trying to do, frequently unsuccessfully?

Don't despair. The advertising and marketing people are trying to create what I call *macro-positions*. A macro-position is a unique vision of a product, service, or company in the collective mind of a large market of thousands or even millions of people.

To win a distinct place in so many minds requires a single compelling vision that's easy to communicate, and there just aren't that many compelling, easy-to-communicate visions to go around in any single market. A hundred soft drinks can't each have a profitable, compelling position. But when a company is lucky or creative enough to find such a position, etching it into millions of minds requires hard work, creativity, disciplined planning and execution, fine art, good luck, and, more often than not, millions of dollars.

Micro-Positioning

Although people like Henry Kissinger, Jimmy Carter, Sylvester Stallone, and Dennis Rodman have established macro-positions in the minds of millions of people, few ordinary Poets can realistically hope to do so. Fortunately, most Poets only need a *micro-position* to be successful. This is a mental picture in the minds of just a few people, perhaps even as few as the single person you're speaking to. Thus a mother has a personal position in the minds of her children, an employee has a personal position in the mind of her boss, a CEO has a personal position in the minds of the board of directors, and a manager has a personal position in the minds of her staff. If your micro-position is a strong, positive one, it becomes far easier to persuade people.

You don't create a micro-position for yourself through advertising, public relations, and celebrity endorsements. You use laserlike focus and consistent communication. Specifically, you must answer the questions "Who are you?" and "What do you want me to believe about you?"

Your answers to these deceptively simple questions—your personal position—must be *succinct, unambiguous, distinctive*, and *relevant* before you can hope to be persuasive.

Succinct means short and precise. People have very short attention spans when it comes to processing information about others.

Unambiguous means that everyone who hears your short position statement should understand it as you intend, without further elaboration. If your personal position is ambiguous, people assign their own meanings, and these meanings may be very different from those you wish to convey.

Distinctive means that your personal position allows listeners to distinguish you from others.

To be relevant, your personal position must answer the question "What can you do for me?" It must cause the people you're trying to persuade to believe you can help them meet their personal needs.

Use the following guidelines to develop your personal position.

Personal Positioning Guidelines

1. Use fifty words or less. After fifty words, communication effectiveness decreases exponentially as the number of words increases. "I've published three books on bankruptcy law and am recognized as one of the country's leading experts," is a powerful personal positioning statement for a bankruptcy lawyer, and it's only sixteen words. "As your father, I want you to know that I'll give you all the emotional and financial support I can to help you do whatever you want to do with your life, no questions asked or strings attached," are thirty-eight words that position you unequivocally with your child.

2. Use unambiguous terms. An ambiguous term is open to different interpretations that create different visual pictures in the minds of different people. If you must use an ambiguous term, limit its meaning with specific modifiers. Say, "I'm a Unix programmer specializing in security systems and in protecting companies' programs and data from tampering, fraud, or loss." This is unambiguous. Just saying you're a programmer, or a computer scientist, or even a Unix programmer, is ambiguous.

3. Avoid universal descriptors. Don't use descriptions and adjectives that everyone would use. If you say you're honest, hardworking, a fast learner, loyal, courteous, kind, or good to your mother, you're just saying what anyone else would say.

Because everyone, either explicitly or implicitly, claims the same thing, your claims won't be distinctive or persuasive. Mention that you graduated first in your class instead of saying you're smart, that you're an Eagle Scout or a deacon at your church instead of that you're honest. Tell them you billed 3,000 hours last year instead of saying you're a hard worker.

4. Use only distinctions you can prove. This is a hard one. But people quickly see unprovable assertions for what they usually are, unfounded exaggerations. If you make claims that people don't believe, you undermine your credibility and trustworthiness, and lead them to doubt even your legitimate claims. It's fine to tell the divorce court judge that your children are so important to you that you've changed your job so you can be with them when they come home from school. But it's not fine to tell her you're the best parent in the state. This unprovable exaggeration may seem harmless, but it's not. The judge is less likely to believe you when you tell her you're a better parent than your ex, even if it's true.

5. Don't brag. Everyone likes to talk about personal achievements and the accomplishments of people, institutions, products, services, and family members that in some way make him or her look good. As we'll discuss in chapter 19, a certain amount of this talk helps substantiate your claims. Telling an interviewer you graduated with honors substantiates that you're smart. Talking about the big order your company landed with an important client can decrease the risk others perceive in dealing with your new company.

But, besides the grandparents, no one cares that your daughter is captain of her field hockey team, or that your son sold the most tickets to the Scout clambake. And no one, not even your mother, cares that you broke 90 playing golf or just bought the biggest lawn tractor on the block.

While it's helpful to talk objectively about anything that substantiates your credibility and trustworthiness, there's a fine line between that and bragging. And people know immediately when you're on the wrong side of it. Focus on your listener. Talk about yourself only when you need to make an objective point. Don't brag, boast, swagger, gloat, or crow. Nothing good will come of it.

6. Describe yourself, your ideas, and your services in terms of your listener's personal needs. Your position is relevant only if it relates to your Prospects' personal needs, so you must answer the question all Prospects have: "What's in it for me?" It's far more relevant to your boss if you position yourself as a systems security expert who can protect him from being embarrassed by hackers breaking into the company's system than just to tell him you're a systems security expert.

Be careful that your personal position in your family is relevant to your spouse and children. If your family has you positioned as a hard worker dedicated to your career—sit down, because you're not going to like this—that may not be relevant to their personal needs. I can hear you thinking, "But I'm doing this for them. My work makes it possible for us to live where we live and own what we own." But if your spouse needs companionship and your children need help being accepted by their peers, your position as superprovider is irrelevant to them no matter how much house, car, and other good stuff your earnings buy.

A point to note is that you have a different personal position for different people in your life. To your company's senior executives, you may be a person who can be counted on to meet production deadlines no matter what. To subordinates, you're someone who looks out for employees' economic and workplace needs. To your family, you're a parent whose only interest is his children's happiness and success.

Everyone important to you has different personal needs, and to be relevant to them, your personal position must relate to those different needs. Your teenager can no more relate to your personal position as a company man than your boss can relate to your position as a family man.

Who Are You?

"Who are you?" is the single most important question in gentle persuasion, and perhaps in life generally. Yet when I ask people this apparently simple question and sit back with pen in hand, ready to record the answer, I invariably get a blank stare in return. Typically, people tell me that although they, of course, know who they are, they've never thought to provide a specific answer before. Especially not one that will be written down for all the world to see.

But Poets are intelligent, articulate people, who are not long lost for words. So after some thought, they begin to answer. Their answers are thoughtful, heartfelt, and honest. Unfortunately, from a communications standpoint, they are nearly always ineffective. Let's look at some typical answers.

I'M A PROFESSIONAL

I'm a lawyer [accountant, consultant, systems analyst, investment banker, manager, doctor, engineer, butcher, baker, or candlestick maker].

This favorite response fails three of our four tests for effective communications. Certainly it's succinct—no problem there. But it's not unambiguous, because different people have in their minds different concepts of what, for example, a lawyer is. One listener may think of someone trying cases in court, another of someone preparing contracts, another of someone defending the poor, and still another of someone chasing ambulances.

Nor is it distinctive. Although it distinguishes you from people who aren't lawyers (or accountants, doctors, engineers, etc.), classifying yourself with hundreds of thousands of others is hardly distinctive. A test for distinctiveness is to work backward, to first recite your description of who you are and see if you're one of a few who fit.

Finally, being a member of a profession or a large group is not, from the standpoint of persuasion, relevant. If you're a lawyer talking to someone who actually needs a lawyer, it may be more useful for him to know you're a lawyer than a piano tuner, but it's not much more useful. Your Prospect wants to know if you can meet his specific legal needs: a tax lawyer who can save him money, a corporate lawyer who can take his company public without overcharging, or a public defender who will keep him out of prison. What you are is relevant only if you can meet your Prospect's personal needs.

Another version of this ineffective personal positioning that's popular is, "I'm a good parent [or caring husband, hard worker, loyal employee]."

Again, while succinct, such a position is ambiguous (just what does it mean to work "hard" at an eight-hour-a-day desk job?), not distinctive (don't all parents claim to be good parents?), and irrelevant (what good does it do your employers if you've worked for them for thirty years and never made quota?).

So if you answer the "Who are you?" question in either your personal or business life by describing yourself as a member of any large, socially acceptable group, you're not communicating effectively or persuasively.

I'M A GENERALIZATION

If you think that the question "Who are you?" is too simpleminded, you're right. It implies that you have to summarize all you are into a simple, single-minded, generalized statement that describes the total real you.

That's not what personal positioning is about. It's not about your whole life, not about who you are and what you stand for as an integrated person. Personal positioning is only about effective communication with the specific people or person you're trying to persuade. The trick is not to answer the question "Who are you as a total human being," but to answer "Who are you relative to me specifically and to my specific needs?" The unspoken part of this is "I know you're probably a lot of other things to a lot of other people, but frankly I don't really care, because it has nothing to do with me."

It's almost strange, but if you want people to listen, hear, remember, and be persuaded, when you answer the question "Who are you?," you must think about the person you're talking to more than you think about yourself. If you focus your answer too much on yourself and try to summarize all you are into the answer, what results are generalities, imprecise or vague statements and ideas.

Helen is a businesswoman in her early forties who was reassessing her career when I met her. She'd been successful in her last two jobs, and she held herself in high regard. And rightly so. She was an intelligent, creative, attractive, articulate, and successful person.

But when I asked her who she was and how she wanted people interviewing her for jobs to see her, she prepared the following personal positioning statement:

> I'm a creative problem solver who has successfully organized and grown startup businesses. Enthusiastic by nature, I empower others to believe in and follow a given course. I enjoy developing and executing marketing plans for new products, and I bring organization, discipline, and sound business thinking to any enterprise.

This is the way she honestly saw herself, and every word was 100-percent honest and accurate, without a trace of exaggeration or hyperbole. But from the standpoint of the people she had to persuade, it was not succinct, unambiguous, distinctive, or relevant. It was far too general. Let's look at the statement as others would see it.

Poets love phrases like "I'm a creative problem solver." Unfortunately, from the standpoint of persuasive communication, they're entirely ineffective, like advertising copy about a new and improved product. Even assuming that creative problem solving is relevant to the listener's needs, the question is, creative compared to what? Or, what kinds of problems?

That Helen had successfully organized and grown startup businesses was somewhat more specific, but still left the listener wondering who she was. Was she the hands-on visionary product developer, the financier and guiding board member, or the sales and marketing expert? (She was none of these.) Was her expertise in software, manufacturing, or biotechnology? (It was in none of these.) The description is too general and ambiguous.

Saying you're enthusiastic, like saying you're honest, hardworking, and dependable, is also ineffective. If asked, everyone will make the same claim. Who would ever admit he was apathetic, dishonest, slothful, or unreliable? If you describe yourself in a way that isn't different from the way everyone else describes himself, you're Talking Without Communicating. People won't argue against you, but neither will they be persuaded.

And so it goes with the rest of Helen's description. No effective communication. No sale.

To be persuasive, Helen should drop the generalities and talk specifically to the needs of the people she has to persuade. If she was interviewing at law firms, a truthful and effective personal position could have been, "I'm a lawyer and entrepreneur. Although I know and love the law, I have the proven ability to attract new clients and build a profitable business. Business clients relate to me especially well because I founded and grew my own business and understand the practical business issues they face every day."

If she's interviewing for a CEO position with a recent startup company, her personal position could be, "I'm an entrepreneur with a proven record of developing profitable new software products for health-care companies. I financed, grew, and took public the two companies I founded, and increased my investors' money tenfold."

I'M MY RÉSUMÉ

Matt was head of marketing and sales at a small software firm. His objective was to be hired as CEO by a rapidly growing software vendor. Because he hadn't previously been a general manager, and his current company was not well known, Matt had some serious shortcomings.

In his hotel room the evening before his interview, Matt happened to read a copy of a talk I had given on personal positioning. Because his résumé was the typical multipage listing of his work experience and education, it did not address succinctly who Matt was and specifically how he could fulfill the needs of the people he was scheduled to meet the next day. So that evening Matt prepared the following personal positioning statement:

> I'm an expert at selling complex software to large companies. I understand how large companies think, and how they make buying decisions. I have a proven record of bringing together product management, product development, and sales and marketing groups to work as a unified team to sell to these companies and kill the competition.

This statement positioned him succinctly, unambiguously, and distinctively. Best of all, even though Matt had not previously run a software company, it described exactly what the company's managers were looking for in their new CEO. So his personal position was relevant to his buyers' personal needs.

The next day, instead of repeatedly talking through his two-page résumé, he used this short personal position in all his interviews. Matt still had to prove that he was what he said he was (we'll get to that in the next chapter), but his personal position was succinct, unambiguous, distinctive, and, to the people looking to hire new a CEO for a high-growth software firm, relevant. It specifically addressed his listeners' needs to succeed and win. People paid attention and listened, and he persuaded the recruiter, the management, and the employees that he was the right person. Mission accomplished.

Getting the Words Right

When it comes to personal positioning, words matter—a lot. If you're trying to get a specific message across to a specific person, you can't just say what profession you're trained in, spout vague generalities, or recite your résumé. You've got to think about whom you're talking to and exactly what it is you want them to believe, and you've got to choose your words carefully. If you don't, you'll wind up Talking Without Communicating.

A simple outline to help you organize your ideas and choose your words for your personal positioning statement is:

> For [your Prospect], I [the Prospect's needs you fulfill]."
> Follow this with a short description of the distinctive way
> you fulfill these needs.

For a lawyer working with a long-term client, this could be, "For the executives of Acme Co., I've made it my first priority to help you avoid shareholder suits, but if they occur, I can help you win them. I know exactly what potential plaintiffs will look for if the company's stock falls, and can help you meet your financial objectives for liquidity without allowing yourself to be open to public criticism or lawsuits you might lose."

A particularly strong alternative form of this positioning statement is this:

"For [your Prospect], I'm an expert at [the Prospect's needs you're an expert in fulfilling]," followed by what it is that makes you an expert.

As a lawyer you could say, "I'm an expert at avoiding and winning shareholder lawsuits. No client I've represented has ever had to pay a penny for a shareholder lawsuit that hasn't been covered by insurance. I've made it my first priority to make sure you can fulfill your financial objectives for liquidity without allowing yourself to be open to public criticism or lawsuits you might lose."

You can also use this outline:

"For [your Prospect], I guarantee that I [the Prospect's needs you guarantee to fulfill]," followed by how you can guarantee to fulfill your Prospect's needs.

The lawyer's personal positioning statement would then be, "If you follow my advice, you and the other executives at Acme Co. will never pay a penny to settle shareholder suits not covered by insurance. I've been doing this for twenty years, and none of my clients has ever paid a settlement out of their company's treasury."

With a little work and thought, you can reduce your message to a relatively few words that are succinct, unambiguous, distinctive, and relevant. Your statement quickly positions you in people's minds and lets them know what to think about you.

You can use this same simple outline for all the Prospects in your everyday life as well as in your business life.

• *For your elderly father:* "I guarantee to meet your needs for security by providing you a stable and predictable home where you can always feel wanted, safe, and supported. You can count on me now the way I counted on you when I was growing up."

• *For your boss:* "I'm an expert at delivering systems on time and within budget so you can meet the commitments you make to your boss and be successful. Project teams I've managed haven't missed a budget or a deadline in the past five years."

• *For your teenager:* "I guarantee to support your drive to become a scholar [athlete, musician, artist]. As long as you do your part, you can count on me to work with you and to provide whatever financial and emotional support and resources you need to be successful."

Unerring Consistency

Once you've created a personal position in people's minds that predisposes them to accept you and your ideas, one that helps you get your way in everyday life, the only way to maintain it is with unerring consistency. Everything you say and do must support and be consistent with the personal position you wish to own in people's minds. If you act inconsistently with your personal position, the damage can be dramatic and irreversible.

If you've positioned yourself in your company as someone who cares about your employees, and you reduce employee benefits solely to increase earnings, you're acting inconsistently with your personal position, and it may be lost forever. If your family sees you as a person whose first priority is their needs, an extramarital affair can permanently change their perceptions. If your boss at the bank has a mental picture of you as sensible and conservative, that's the way you should behave at the holiday party.

A positive personal position is a valuable personal asset. Keeping it intact requires constant attention and scrupulously consistent behavior.

Gentle Persuasion Habit No. 16

Position yourself in a way that's succinct, unambiguous, distinctive and relevant. Always act consistently with your personal position.

Okay, you've thought through the personal position you want to own in people's minds. You've written it out, and it's succinct, unambiguous, distinctive, and relevant. You behave consistently with your position. Best of all, it's really you. All you have to do now is get people to believe it's really you. You need a compelling story to substantiate your claim. That, in part, is the topic of the next chapter.

19

Yeah, Says Who?

I'VE ARRIVED AND TO PROVE IT I'M HERE!

—*Max Bygraves*

If I had to choose the best from among all the advice in all the books I've read on selling, the courses I've attended, and the video- and audiotapes I've listened to and watched, it is this one thing that nearly all of them say at one time or another: *"Telling isn't selling."*

Very simply, people don't always believe you just because you've said something. Or at least they don't believe you enough to do what you want them to. Don't take it personally; it happens to certified experts, presidents, and the Pope, as well as to you.

There are a number of reasons for this. First, people might believe you're not being forthright and are trying to mislead them. If this is the problem, you haven't established a perception of trustworthiness, and the job of getting your way is going to be tough.

But even if people trust you, they still may not believe you. Not being believed is a state in between being believed and being disbelieved. It's a subtle but important distinction, because until your Prospect actually believes you, you won't get your way.

Your Prospect may trust but not believe you because of one of the following factors:

•He may be facing competing requests from others he considers equally trustworthy. Everyone's trying to convince him, and he doesn't know whom to believe. (You and your teenager's friends at school may be giving him very different advice. He trusts both of you and believes you both have his best interests at heart. So while he doesn't disbelieve what you tell him, neither does he believe it enough to ignore his friends' advice and do what you want him to do.)

•She may believe you're trustworthy, but feel you're not competent enough to give her the best advice. This often happens in competitive situations when people feel you don't really understand their other options. (If you're a nonsmoker trying to persuade your child to stop smoking, she knows you're motivated by her best interests, but she's not persuaded because she also knows you don't understand the pleasure she gets from smoking, or how difficult it is to quit. If you're trying to persuade a prospective client to use your legal services, he may believe you're competent and trustworthy, but fail to be persuaded by your proposal because you don't understand the value his current law firm provides.)

•He may worry that, although you're trustworthy, you have something to gain by his believing you or accepting your proposal, and this influences your advice. Thus he discounts your opinions about competing alternatives, even though he doesn't question your trustworthiness. (My wife may love and trust me, but there's no way I'll persuade her it will be more fun to ride cross-country on the back of a motorcycle than to spend two weeks in Paris.)

• Like everyone else, he's suffering from selling and marketing overload. Having been bombarded by sales efforts trying to convince him of things during his every waking hour, he's hardened to all appeals simply out of self-defense.

• What you're proposing is at odds with his past experiences, biases, and preconceived notions. I have no doubt my daughter trusts me. But she's learned from past experiences that she *really* dislikes biking. Despite her implicit trust in me, nothing I say will persuade her she'll enjoy a biking vacation.

This is a long and impressive list of reasons that someone won't believe what you say, or do what you ask even if he trusts you. So how do you get someone to believe you enough to do what you want him to do? One way is to *prove that what you're saying is true.*

People form their opinions about the truth of something through *supporting evidence, references, and experiences.* You must weave all three into a seamless story that substantiates the claims you make about yourself, your ideas, or your services. This is your *substantiating story,* and it should be as carefully thought out as your personal position.

Supporting Evidence

Don't sell yourself short. Anything that supports the veracity of your claims is valuable evidence for your substantiating story. If you're like most people, you'll tend to focus on the issue of the moment—your current job, your recent professional experience, the courses you just took. But you can call on anything from your entire life to help make a convincing case. Look for your most impressive and relevant accomplishments and include them in your substantiating story. That you were valedictorian of your high-school graduating class is as convincing evidence of intelligence for an eighty-year-old as it would be if you were just graduating from college at twenty-one.

I interviewed a job candidate who scored 1600 on his SATs, the highest possible score. Although SATs may be totally irrelevant to what people do in real life, there's no denying that a perfect score is an impressive and unusual accomplishment, and convincing evidence of intelligence. The candidate managed to work this accomplishment casually into the conversation during the interview.

Even though our interview occurred over twenty-five years after his SATs, his score was more effective in proving his intelligence than anything on his résumé. He wasn't bragging, but was simply stating a fact that he worked naturally into the conversation. It was the evidence I used to infer his intelligence without his having to say another word on the topic.

It doesn't matter what you want your Prospect to believe: that you're a good manager, an effective leader, religious, family-oriented, a great salesperson, creative; that you inspire loyalty from clients or employees; that you're a financial guru, an engineering genius, or a great writer. You must prove your claim, and one way to do that is to create an evidence list from your entire life that you weave into a substantiating story that incontrovertibly proves your points. But remember, no bragging.

Negative Evidence

While you're working to build a preponderance of positive evidence supporting your claims, people may also learn of negative evidence that works against you. Such evidence may come from a competitor, but it's typically present even in non-competitive situations.

Your Prospect may know an unhappy client, or may not think highly of your alma mater or your previous employers; you may have been fired from your last job, lost a case, or failed to close an important account. Life is a series of ups and downs, and you'll get your share of downs that are visible enough to affect people's opinions of you.

So what? People with front-page failures recover to become successful again. To recover from the effects of negative evidence, you must not only develop positive evidence to support your claims, but you must also present logical, credible, strong arguments that show why the negative evidence shouldn't be held against you.

Say you need to prove your intelligence, but you attended third-rate schools that you suspect don't impress the interviewer. The wrong approach, which is most people's instinct, is to defend the school by building it into more than it is. You proclaim that it is one of the ten best schools in southern Boondocks County for tax law, or that it has a great, dedicated faculty. Even if it's true, it's counter to your listener's beliefs and without strong proof. The interviewer will smile and nod but won't be persuaded.

I interviewed an engineer who handled the question of his education far better. He began by stating what I believed, that the schools he attended were not especially good ones. He said he'd compensated by working hard and graduating near the top of his class, but he did not try to build the schools into more than I believed they were.

But he went on to tell me that, owing to his family circumstances, he'd had to make his way through undergraduate and graduate school on his own, and the state schools he'd attended were all he could afford. This explanation countered the negative evidence leading me to believe he wasn't smart enough to be accepted by higher-rated schools.

He then turned his attention to his accomplishments in graduate school and immediately after. They were impressive, clear evidence of his intelligence and drive. He turned out to be one of the best engineers I ever hired, indeed one of the best people I've ever hired for any job. But I wouldn't have hired him if he hadn't made the sale.

You're Fired!

Being fired from your last job is always a concern to your next employer. Interviewers wonder why you really lost your job, and worry that the firing may be an indication of hidden problems. Without making excuses or blaming others, it's essential that you answer this negative evidence. The best approach is to be positive, even with the most negative events. *Being negative about anything is almost always a losing strategy in persuasion.*

How you handle a negative situation like a firing depends far more on what positive claim you want to prove than on the negative event you want to explain. Follow these steps:

• *Admit positively.* If the negative evidence is true, admit to it in the most positive way possible. "I was fired, and although I didn't realize it at the time, it was the best thing that could have happened to me." Or, "I was fired and it was the worst thing that happened to me in my career, because I loved the company and all the people and customers I worked with."

• *Explain positively.* Without giving excuses, logically explain the special circumstances behind the negative event. These must be strong, credible, and logical reasons why the Prospect's beliefs are incorrect. Your tone must be positive. "The products I was selling were great, and the people who built and serviced them were dedicated, but the underlying technology changed and the product became outdated. It wasn't something that was easy for the company's management to foresee, but it left me with a product that was nearly impossible to sell, even though the market was growing. Management had no choice but to sell the company. The new owner had its own management team, so we were all let go after the merger."

• *Move on positively.* Move on to the current situation with positive evidence supporting your positive claims. "The experience forced me to motivate salespeople under difficult circumstances. Even though the market moved away from the company's technology and the company was up for sale, I held the old team together and kept sales steady while they looked for someone to buy the company. Anyone can sell a great product into a growing market. This taught me to sell a weak product against tough competitors. It was a difficult period, but now I'm ready for the next challenge."

References

A special kind of evidence is references, credible people willing to attest to your claims. Credibility refers to the believability of your references, which is determined by who's giving the reference, what they're attesting to, and whether people perceive them as honest and impartial.

The head of the World Bank may have great credibility in many things, but not if he were attesting to, say, the effectiveness of STP engine oil additive; a NASCAR driver with an eighth-grade education would be more credible. The head of a Fortune 100 company might be a credible business reference for you, but not if he's your father. People won't believe he's impartial.

Work to get the best references you can, but don't expect too much from them. They're useful only to the extent that they help you support your personal position and prove your competence and trustworthiness. References substantiate, they don't sell. Certainly they don't take the place of a compelling personal position.

I interviewed Jack for a senior management position. He came to the interview armed with a set of written references from past employers, several with industry-known, impressive names. He presented them to me as a Russian nobleman would present a letter of reference from a grand duke to a general in the tsar's army. He believed that his strong references would persuade me of his worth. But to be persuasive, references should prove something of specific interest to the buyer besides simply the fact that the seller has references.

Much to Jack's consternation, I wasn't interested in reading his references, and refused to do so. I wanted to learn from him in his own words how he could meet my needs. Only toward the end of the hiring process did I personally call his references, looking only to confirm that the opinions I had formed about Jack were accurate. I never read his prefab written references.

No References? No Problem

Finally, don't despair if you don't have good references. References are only one of three ways to substantiate claims, and they're not always necessary to persuade successfully. If other compelling evidence is available, or if you can use the techniques of the next chapter to provide people with personal experiences, references become less important.

This is especially good news for people beginning a new career, practice, or business who haven't yet established credible references. No business had a good reference before it won its first account, and no employee had a good reference before her first job. All relied on other evidence for the first sale. And good people who have had the misfortune, for whatever reason, to have a number of unfavorable references can still sell themselves successfully.

Curb Your Claims

What if, when you're creating your evidence list, you can't find anything that attests to what you want your listener to believe? No references, no credible evidence, no personal experiences you can provide people. You probably won't like what I'm going to tell you next, but *if you can't compile compelling evidence to a claim, you shouldn't make it.*

It doesn't matter how important you may feel the claim is, you won't be credible to your listener. Instead, concentrate on positive characteristics you can prove, characteristics your listeners can infer from credible, convincing evidence and experiences you provide.

The same advice applies when you're talking about your services, whether they're in law, accounting, investment banking, executive recruiting, financial planning, medicine, or lawn care. *Be prepared to provide evidence of any claim you make. Don't make any claim you can't substantiate either with convincing evidence or through references or experiences* (which we'll discuss shortly). This is a difficult discipline to maintain, but if you violate it, you won't be credible. You won't communicate effectively.

Alex, a commercial real-estate broker specializing in tenant representation, called on me when my company needed new office space. He made two claims as part of his presentation: that he would provide me with superior service and that he would work hard on my behalf.

Alex was sincere, well-spoken, experienced in the industry, and presented himself and his firm well. But he neither substantiated his claims nor had them well defined. He could not explain what he meant when he said he would work hard on my behalf. Could I really believe Alex would work harder than his equally sincere competitors? Nor could he explain what superior services he would provide, compared with his competitors. Making claims he couldn't substantiate hurt his credibility in my eyes.

I liked Alex and wanted him to win my business, but he couldn't convince me, even though I wanted to be convinced. He lacked the evidence that could substantiate an unambiguous, meaningful distinction in his services. Saying he would provide superior service and work hard for me without substantiating his claims was Talking Without Communicating. Empty words. No sale.

On the other hand, his competitor, Ron, came well prepared. He also claimed he'd provide me with superior service. When I asked specifically what that meant, Ron was ready with a meaningful answer, complete with evidence to substantiate it.

Instead of pounding his chest and telling me how hard he'd work to sublease our existing space and find us new offices, he instead admitted that when it came to leasing and subleasing, one broker was about as good as any other. But what his firm could do that others couldn't was help us plan and manage the transition to new quarters so that our move took place within a predictable budget and schedule. This was a meaningful, relevant distinction, because predictability was essential if I was to keep my board of directors and the people working for the company happy.

Now all Ron had to do was substantiate his claim and address my buying anxieties. He did this by assuring me that because his firm had its own architectural and construction management group, it had the long-term relationships with subcontractors that could guarantee the project would be completed within the time frame and budget we agreed upon. This was of particular concern to me because, at the time when we were looking to relocate, the real-estate market was white-hot, and overcommitted subcontractors often promised more than they could deliver.

To be able to credibly guarantee that things will go as a Prospect plans is compelling. The morale and attitude of every employee in our office would have been hurt if the move went badly, and the company's management would have looked incompetent or insensitive. Although Ron's company started with a disadvantage (because of my own prior biases), good preparation and communications, in the form of a precise positioning statement and a credible substantiating story, won the day and made the sale.

Gentle Persuasion Habit No. 17

Telling isn't selling. Collect evidence and references and weave them into a credible substantiating story that proves your claims.

20

Show and Tell

WE ARE GENERALLY BETTER PERSUADED BY THE
REASONS WE DISCOVER OURSELVES THAN BY THOSE
GIVEN TO US BY OTHERS.

—*Blaise Pascal*

Think about the last time you were on the receiving end of a sales presentation. It could have been at work, over the phone, in a store, or during a conversation with a friend or family member.

You knew the person doing the talking was out to "present" whatever he was selling, and to put it in the most favorable light. From the start, you didn't believe the presentation would be objective, that it would highlight strengths and weaknesses alike and give competing options equal consideration. So, knowing the presenter wasn't objective and impartial, you weren't ready to accept his facts, evidence, logic, arguments, and assurances. There's a good chance your instinct was to question everything, including facts and reasoning you'd have accepted readily under other conditions. You might even have come to the discussion armed with counterarguments and a determination not to be sold.

I remember walking into a car dealership with the express

intention of buying the latest model of an SUV I'd owned for six years and driven for 90,000 carefree, horse-trailer-pulling, kid-hauling, chore-doing, vacation-taking miles. We loved the truck, but it was time to trade it in before it became costly to maintain and its value plummeted.

I had called ahead to be sure the dealer had the vehicle I wanted in stock, and we were met by the salesman I'd talked to on the phone. He was a rail-thin, well-dressed man in his very early twenties, who would best be described as exuberant. But this was not to be his finest hour.

He knew exactly what model we were interested in, and from the beginning handshake and smile, he started to sell, giving us a sales presentation about all the vehicle's features and benefits. Now, I'd done the research on competing SUVs, so I knew more about the alternatives than did the salesman, who knew his own company's products well, but little else.

Our conversation was a sort of out-of body experience. My wife and I both watched in stunned amazement as I, reacting only to the salesman and his presentation and not according to our plans, disputed every point he made. He told me the truck was known for its reliability. I said, "Sure, it's also known for its high maintenance cost." He told me how well the truck held its value, and I countered that while that might be true in percentage terms, in terms of dollars, a competing brand was cheaper.

I knew all the trade-offs before I'd decided to replace my SUV with the new model, and actually went to the store hoping I could buy the new truck and be done with it. But I knew the salesman wasn't objective and wasn't giving me a balanced presentation, so I fought him on every point. Much to my wife's surprise—and mine—I won. I talked myself out of buying the truck I'd intended to buy, the truck we'd talked about buying for almost a year. Instead, we went to another dealer and bought another company's more expensive model.

This is the fatal flaw of classic sales presentations: *Conversations or meetings that occur for the specific purpose of persuasion are perfectly structured not to be persuasive.* Remember the First Law of Persuasion: Every persuasive force causes an opposite resisting force. No wonder Poets hate to make sales pitches.

Still, there will be times when you won't have a choice. You're calling on a prospective client and everyone knows it's for the purpose of winning the client's business. You have a job interview, and you're there for only one reason—to sell yourself. You're making a presentation to the boss to get approval for a new project. You've just returned from the Porsche dealership, and your spouse knows exactly what's on your mind.

Fortunately, there's a persuasion strategy for these situations that's ideally suited to Poets and to gentle persuasion. Instead of giving a "presentation," it's based on the idea of giving people a personal experience with what you're selling.

Personal Experiences

Why are schoolchildren forced to dissect frogs? Whatever there is to learn from the inside of a frog can be taught out of textbooks with well-worded descriptions and vivid color photographs. Since few students subjected to the frog-dissecting ritual will ever be required in life to dissect anything beyond a pizza, the exercise seems to be a waste of limited educational time and money—to say nothing of the price paid by the frogs.

Children dissect frogs for the same reason they go on field trips, which is the same reason perfume ladies spray department store shoppers, Amway leaves samples with customers, and car salespeople let prospects they've never seen before take $50,000 cars for test drives. They do it because personal experiences capture and hold people's attention, get them involved and thinking, and make them remember—the essential elements of persuasive communication.

When it comes to persuasion, the multisense, full body-and-mind involvement of personal experiences beats facts, logic, references, evidence, arguments, and expert opinions ten to one. Personal experiences work because they keep you fully engaged, paying attention, and processing information. When you're only listening or watching, this may not be the case at all. More than that, when you personally experience something, you form opinions without depending on others whose motives may be suspect.

So, while providing compelling evidence is far more persuasive than simply telling, personal experiences can be far more persuasive than even compelling evidence. And when you're short of compelling evidence, it might be the only way you'll be persuasive.

That's why good car salespeople don't depend on testimonials and oral descriptions of technical facts to sell. Instead they put you behind the wheel and let you drive the car. You bask in the luxury of a new car with its new-car smell, or burn a little rubber in the parking lot as soon as the salesperson isn't looking. Your personal experience is far more effective than all the spoken or written words in forming your beliefs and perceptions.

Poets are surprised to learn that *giving people this same kind of personal experience is the single most effective way to sell themselves, their ideas, and their services, especially when they have had little or no previous relationship with their Prospect.* To understand why, put yourself in your Prospect's shoes.

You're listening to a proposal from someone you don't know from Yoda. You have no idea whether he can fulfill your needs, but everything will depend on him. Despite everything he and his references say, a lot can go wrong when success depends on someone you don't really know. The personal chemistry may not be right, his experience or knowledge may be insufficient, he may charge too much or not provide the quality of service he says he'll give.

None of this plays to the strengths of selling Poets, who typically have difficulty uncovering personal needs and buying anxieties, and addressing them effectively. Even when Poets understand people's underlying concerns, they often can't find the proof they need to be persuasive.

What evidence and references can you come up with to assure a prospective client that you'll work well together, to persuade your kids that they'll fit in at the school in their new town, or to convince an interviewer that you'll be fun to work with? Some things in life just can't be proved objectively, even when you're successful at getting people to pay attention and think about what you're saying.

If a big part of what you're selling is yourself—your ideas, your ability to lead, your candidacy for a job—give people personal experiences with what you're selling. There are two ways to do this. You can vividly describe *past* experiences to which people can personally relate, or you can talk to people during your presentation in a way that allows them to experience personally what it will be like working with you in the *future*.

Vivid Storytelling

Human beings are story-loving creatures. Even children and adults who normally have no tolerance for sitting still and listening will listen to and remember an interesting, relevant, and vivid story. But the key word is *vivid*, which means to *evoke lifelike images that are heard, seen, or felt as if they were real.*

Vivid stories work for the same reason personal experiences work. If you can vividly portray images and emotions in stories you tell about yourself, your ideas, or your services, you help people share an experience vicariously. It can be as effective as having been there.

Alice was a New York City–based computer systems consultant bidding on an assignment to build and install an order-processing system for a Midwest-headquartered division of a Fortune 200 company. Professionally, Alice was a product of the information age—expert and confident with technology, and a heads-down, no-nonsense project manager for whom missing systems development budgets or time schedules were mortal sins, things you just don't do.

Personally, she was in her early thirties, single, and with

interpersonal skills that were a little rough around the edges. She tended to be brusque, all business, and impatient with people (including the client's staff) who didn't live up to her standards. She carried just enough of a New York City attitude and accent so that most Midwesterners would guess she was from out of town—far out of town—thirty seconds into the first conversation.

The Prospects she was meeting were the company's division manager, the corporate head of information services, several systems project managers, and a half-dozen people who would eventually use the system. They were products of a nuts-and-bolts manufacturing business—competent, hardworking, conservative, salt-of-the-earth, Midwest businessmen who tolerated computers but didn't particularly like them.

Although it wasn't obvious to a casual observer, or to anyone in the meeting, Alice and her Prospects were well matched professionally and temperamentally. They were all work oriented, bottom-line driven, and competent at what they did. But the personal fit was strictly the Odd Couple.

Alice understood that calling in an outsider to build a core business system was an emotionally charged, anxiety-intensive decision. The division manager worried about whether the system would be completed as planned, whether it would support the business adequately even if completed successfully, and whether costs would be as predicted. Users worried about learning new procedures, changes to their lives, and threats to their job security if the system didn't perform. The technology people worried about job security because of outsiders doing work they were hired to do, about loss of status, and about maintaining the systems after the consultants left.

And, although no one dared talk about it, Alice also suspected the group was worried about a young, New York City–based woman being in charge of such a complex systems project.

Alice's challenge was to persuade people with whom she appeared to have little in common that she and her team could work with the Prospect's team to build and install the most complex system the division had ever built. She had never received a day of sales training, but she was competent and trustworthy, she truly cared about her customers, and her instincts were good.

At the presentation, Alice began by asking if it would help if she described how she and her staff had worked with the people building a similar system for another client. Of course, her prospects agreed. (Her question told the group she would tell them a relevant story, and introduced an element of mystery, so she easily won their attention.)

She then described how she and her staff had worked with her other client. The story was a series of vignettes and anecdotes to which people in the meeting could relate. Alice didn't try to portray her company as flawless implementers working in an idyllic relationship with the client. Instead she described realistic problems and issues that arise in any systems project, and ways in which she and her client's people had worked together, occasionally less than elegantly but always effectively, to find solutions.

Alice's story covered issues she knew were on her Prospects' minds: approval of system specifications, staff turnover during the project, changes to specifications, cost increases, performance issues, maintenance staff training. The story reflected real-world experience, and was amusing and balanced in the telling.

When it was over, the listeners felt as if they had experienced what it was like to work with Alice and her team. They could visualize their needs being met and their concerns answered, because they had vicariously shared a similar experience. Any concerns they had about Alice vanished. When they agreed to go ahead with the project, one of their requirements was that Alice be assigned as team leader.

The same thing happened when my son considered going to Boy Scout summer camp for the first time. Using standard Kid

Logic, he decided, based on a total lack of information, that it would be "boring and dumb," and he wasn't going.

Now, every male who has gone to Boy Scout camp knows it was a defining experience in his life. A front-page *Wall Street Journal* article once theorized that the secret objective of all male CEOs is to re-create their Boy Scout camp experience in their companies. (I thought this was a remarkable insight, because the previous week I had signed a lease on new company office space. I actually told my CFO I'd chosen the office park because it reminded me of the Boy Scout camp I'd attended.)

So Dad Logic resolved that my son would go to Boy Scout camp. I persuaded him with my vivid stories about swimming, canoe fights, camp songs, bug juice, huge bonfires, ghost stories, good friends, and weeks of high-testosterone, guy-intensive freedom. It worked. He decided to go. (When he returned, his first words on seeing us were, "That was the funnest camp ever." Phew.)

Telling stories to share experiences with your Prospect is easy to do and very effective. The only requirements are that the story be true, well balanced without self-aggrandizement, and told in an interesting or amusing way so it captures your listeners' attention and imagination.

If you're not a natural storyteller, don't wing it. Think through the stories beforehand, practice them out loud, use them whenever appropriate. Practice will make you as good as you have to be.

The Test Drive

In the examples recounted above, Alice and I told vivid stories so our Prospects could share *past* experiences. But it's even more effective if people can have a personal experience with the *future*. Interestingly, it's often easier to help people experience their own future than to have them experience someone else's past. You don't even have to be a good storyteller to do it.

Car salespeople take you for a test drive so you can project yourself into the future and sense what it will be like to own the car. Consumer goods companies give you free samples. Art galleries let you take art home to hang on your wall before you decide. You can do the same thing. You can project your Prospect into the future so that she personally experiences what it will be like if she decides to let you get your way.

Bob was a CEO candidate at a small technology company. He was scheduled to interview with eight people, ranging from board members to people who'd be working for him.

If for no other reason than that he wanted to avoid the boredom of having the same conversation eight times in a single day, Bob resolved that he wasn't going to review his résumé with each interviewer, which was what would have happened in the normal course of events. Instead, without being presumptuous, he approached each meeting as if he and the interviewer were already working together.

When Bob met with Joan, the chief financial officer, he summarized his background in two minutes by simply describing his last job and how he had led the company to increased sales. This was just enough information to position him in Joan's mind as the successful CEO of a high-growth company. He didn't discuss his career before his last job, his education, his references, his family and personal life, or his plans and aspirations.

Instead he asked the CFO what she believed her biggest challenges were. It so happened that the company's obsolete accounting systems were making it impossible for her to do her job well. She admitted being frazzled and stressed by not being able to respond to requests for information from senior managers and board members. She'd continually asked for the money to upgrade the systems, but it was a costly exercise, and because the company's future was uncertain, the board wouldn't approve the project.

Bob knew nothing about accounting systems, but he responded as if he were already the CEO and Joan was bringing this problem to him for his help. Bob and Joan spent almost the entire interview talking about the company's financial planning and reporting needs, and about what options were available to solve the CFO's problems. They talked about the disadvantages of struggling along with the existing system versus the costs and operational hassles of buying and converting to a new system. In the end they agreed that if the company wasn't going to be sold, upgrading the accounting systems would have to be a top priority. Until then, Joan could make do with an extra temporary accountant.

She didn't have to guess what it would be like working with Bob—she had a personal experience, even though it had lasted only forty-five minutes. She enthusiastically recommended hiring him.

And so it went with the other meetings. In the eight interviews and seven hours of discussions, Bob spent no more than fifteen minutes talking about himself, his background, and his qualifications. He used the rest of the time to give his interviewers vivid personal experiences so that they'd know what it would be like working with him. He gave eight test drives. The recommendations came in eight to zero, and he was hired.

This same selling strategy works just as effectively for interviewers as for job seekers. In his book *All Too Human*, George Stephanopoulos describes how Bill Clinton persuaded him to join his first presidential campaign.

> [H]e asked me for my advice. . . . For the next half hour, I joined him on the first of countless stream-of-consciousness tours across the political landscape of his mind. He seemed to know something about everything. . . . He asked me about the 1990 budget deal, one of my areas of expertise. What was good about it? Where was it weak? . . . *He wasn't testing me, just looking for advice*, and it seemed as if he was taking it in, filing it away for future use. *We were working*

together from the moment we met. . . . It was how I felt around him: uniquely known and needed, as if my contribution might make all the difference. [Emphasis added.]

Stephanopoulos had also interviewed with Senator Bob Kerry, with whom he had more in common politically, and who was ahead in the polls at the time. But in a single meeting, Clinton gave Stephanopoulos a vivid test drive and persuaded this valuable staffer to join his campaign and not Kerry's.

To create this personal experience for people, view your discussions not as presentations but as performances, performances that help people visualize you fulfilling their needs and that answer their buying anxieties. Create and rehearse a miniscreenplay that projects people into a realistic personal experience with you, an experience that predisposes them to believe what you're telling them. It's a sophisticated version of show-and-tell, played for high stakes.

Stripped of all the romantic folderol, test drives are all that's behind dating and engagements before marriage. Single people can't provide objective evidence and references that can assure their prospective partner what married life will be like. A woman doesn't call her fiancé's mother, priest, parole officer, or ex-wife. A man doesn't ask for references from his intended bride's sorority sisters, father, and old boyfriends. Instead, both form their beliefs about their future married life based on their personal dating experiences. And while they're having their own personal experiences trying to visualize the future, they're working to create the most positive, persuasive personal experience for their partner.

So, if you don't have hard evidence to substantiate a compelling personal position, and if you're dealing with someone you can't persuade based just on your competence, trustworthiness, and unquestioned belief that you put their interests first, test drives are your most potent persuasion strategy. If what you're proposing is right for your Prospects, they'll see this for themselves after their test drive. It's an open, honest, and effective approach that helps you get your way without compromising your principles and without causing the buying resistance that's otherwise the natural response to being persuaded.

Continuous Positive Reinforcement

All this sounds great, and it is, until people get to know you, really know you, for better or for worse. Then the rules change.

You may be a professional bidding on follow-on business from a client you've served since he started his company; an employee trying to get the guy for whom you've worked for the past five years to approve a proposal; a writer selling a new concept to your old agent; or a parent helping your child choose a college.

In an established relationship, your Prospect already knows what to expect when dealing with you. You don't need to create a vivid experience, because whatever you say is inconsequential compared with your Prospect's past experiences with you. *The only way to continually get your way with people with whom you have an ongoing relationship is to consistently reward them for being persuaded.*

I had a sales manager who worked for me for years, and for years he'd make me crazy. I was trying to build a company with predictable growth achieved through disciplined selling, and every quarter he'd bring me creative deals that required special attention, special contracts with unique terms and conditions, and special relationships with customers. The deals almost always required my participation to close and approve, so he was always trying to persuade me to do something I really didn't want to do, and wouldn't do for other sales managers.

But he never failed me. For example, he told me that if I canceled a family ski vacation and met with an important contingent of executives who were going to be in town in the middle of the same week I was planning to be in the mountains, he'd close an important sale. My family only skis one week a year, we plan the trip nearly a year ahead of time, and we look forward to it. To say I wasn't happy with his request doesn't begin to describe my reaction. Nevertheless, I agreed, and incurred a large cancellation penalty and the wrath of my family.

But he delivered the sale, a very significant one for the company. This same sort of thing happened every quarter. If I'd agree to something—to a lower price, to assign extra people, to make a new customer head of a user committee—he'd guarantee to do something the company needed to have done. And he did. He continuously reinforced me for being persuaded, so he continued to be able to persuade me.

This was in stark contract to the sales manager who ran one of the company's other regions and who was always just a little short of quota. Although I personally liked and trusted the man, he couldn't persuade me. Because he hadn't consistently delivered on previous promises, I was reluctant to agree to anything he asked for without first consulting others.

This is the way life works. If you do what you say you're going to do, you'll find it easy to get your way with people who know you. But the road to hell is paved with good intentions, and keeping people happy with you is harder than it sounds. Every contact with the people in your life should be a positive experience for them, and this doesn't happen without planning and effort. Return calls promptly, answer questions honestly, keep all your promises, provide superior service, bill your clients so they always feel they somehow won a little something, be there for your daughter's school play.

When the people you deal with at work and at home receive continuous positive reinforcement dealing with you, they'll seek you out. Getting your way in everyday life will be easy. When you've reached this point with all your clients, associates, and family members, you can put aside this book, because you'll get your way without any extra effort. You'll be persuasive just because you're you. Just like George Bailey.

Gentle Persuasion Habits Nos. 18 and 19

- *To persuade people who don't know you, or to sell new ideas, give a test drive.*
- *With everyone, always keep your promises, do what you say you're going to do, and make them happy that they let you get your way.*

21

How Nice Guys
Finish First

THERE HE SITS, LIKE A VERY OLD BEAST OF THE
JUNGLE OR VELDT, TURNING HIS GREAT SAD EYES
NOW THIS WAY, NOW THAT, IN AN ATTEMPT TO
LOCATE HIS ENEMIES, AND CONTEMPLATING THE
WHILE WHETHER TO TAKE EVASIVE ACTION OR
MOUNT A COUNTERATTACK.

—*Alan Watkins*

Sometimes in everyday life it's just you alone with your
Prospects, listening, thinking, responding, and trying to get
your way. But often there's someone else lurking—your competition. Then, like it or not, getting your way requires that
you prevent someone else from getting their way.

In everyday life, competitors can be professionals calling on
your clients, job candidates applying for the same job, other
department heads vying for limited funding, or your children's
peers pressuring them to drink or smoke. While your Prospects
listen to you and consider your proposal, they're also influenced by competing options and proposals. So what are you
going to do about it?

Research shows that the way you treat your competitors can
make a big difference in your persuasiveness and whether
you'll get your way. The right strategy depends on what you
and your Prospect know about your competitors. There are
three possibilities: You know about competitors but your

Prospect doesn't (or has simply decided not to consider competitors he knows about); your Prospect is considering competitors whose proposals you know about; or your Prospect is considering competitors whose proposals you don't know about.

We'll call these three situations *sole source, known competition,* and *blind competition,* respectively. Sole source and blind competition share the same strategies, although for different reasons. Known competition requires a very different competitive strategy from the other two.

Sole Source

It often happens that you have competitors, but your Prospect may be unaware of them, or for good reasons, may elect not to consider them. Longtime clients you've serviced well for years may know there are many excellent professional firms competing with yours, but may choose not to have them bid on every new piece of business.

The strategy for dealing with competitors in this situation is easy to follow: Ignore them completely. It's not effective to talk about why you can do a better job than options your Prospect isn't considering, even if your arguments are compelling. If your arguments aren't compelling, you risk inflicting serious persuasive damage.

Unfortunately, Poets too often talk when they shouldn't. When my wife and daughter and I were searching for a school for my daughter, we listened to the dean of a girls' school we visited talk to interested students and parents. Because of the school's location and reputation, and the large number of openings available for ninth-grade girls, top students were reasonably sure of admittance, and many families applied to the school without applying to others. That was our original intent, and we talked for more than a year about the school as if attending were a foregone conclusion.

But the dean began his talk by telling us, "There are many

fine schools open to girls like your daughter." He named names and spoke highly of them, his objective being to position his school in the same group.

We came into the meeting predisposed to favor his school and not intending to research schools outside our immediate area. But after his talk, our reaction was, "Hey, wait a minute. Maybe we need to look into those other options." The end result was that even though my daughter was finally admitted to the school we visited, we seriously considered and then chose a competing school I had never heard of before listening to the dean's talk.

Known Competition

When both you and your Prospect know about competing alternatives, you have three possible strategies: You can ignore your competitors, acknowledge them but ignore the specifics of their arguments, or acknowledge them and specifically refute their arguments.

Contrary to most Poets' instincts, the best strategy is not to ignore your competitors and politely focus only on your own proposal. By far the best strategy is to refute your competitor's arguments knowledgeably and constructively, in a fair and positive way.

This strategy works best for several reasons. First, if you know the options your Prospect is considering, your Prospect will perceive you as competent, which we know increases persuasiveness. If you're fair and not negative (which is not the same as being positive), you'll be perceived as trustworthy, again important for persuasiveness.

But most importantly, your knowledgeable, fair arguments against your competitors' proposals will help your Prospect form his own thoughts about your competitors. Although you may thoroughly understand why your proposal is demonstrably superior to your competitors', don't assume your Prospect has been able to reach the same conclusion.

He may be confused, not know all the facts, be unintentionally or purposefully misled by your competitors, or just not be clever enough to do a competent comparison on his own. If you can do it for him, and if you can do it fairly and without becoming negative, you should. If you don't, perhaps from a misguided belief that it's somehow wrong to talk about your competition, there's a good chance you won't get your way. The result: Both you and your Prospect will suffer.

How do you attack your competition and still remain the principled person everyone thinks you are? I wanted to persuade the father of my son's best friend to have his son join the Boy Scout troop my son was joining. I knew they were leaning toward a different troop.

In addition to sharing the reasons we picked our troop, I described the chaotic meeting I saw when I visited the other troop, and explained why I felt that that environment would not meet our sons' needs. My arguments against the other troop won the day, not my arguments for our selected troop. He did not think poorly of me for knowledgeably, fairly, and constructively sharing my objective observations.

If the dean at the school we were considering for my daughter believed many families were considering competing schools, he could have helped us understand why his school was a better choice. For example, one of the school's competitive advantages was a program that required every student to work one day a week in a meaningful government or public service job during her last three high-school years. One part of the dean's presentation could have been:

"Our requirement that each girl work in a government or public service program provides life training they can't get from other public or private schools." This highlights a competitive distinction. It doesn't just say, "Here's something we do." It says, "Here's something we do to fulfill your daughter's personal needs that our competitors don't do."

As substantiating proof for the claim that this competitive difference meets important personal needs, he could then have followed up with: "The students and alumnae who'll speak next will tell you how important this experience was to their success in college acceptances and after graduation."

This is a positive, fair, and knowledgeable approach that nevertheless attacks competing schools head-on. It is a principled assault on the competition.

Refuting competitive arguments is significantly more effective in persuasion than ignoring competitors or talking about them but not refuting their arguments. One study found that arguments presenting and refuting competitors' proposals were 20 percent more effective than arguments ignoring competitive proposals. On the other hand, arguments acknowledging competitors' positions but *not* refuting them were 20 percent *less* effective than arguments that ignored competitors. That's a 40-percent difference between the best and worst strategies for dealing with competitors!

This is a startling result, because if you're like most Poets, your instinct is to favor the least effective strategy—to acknowledge competitors but focus on your own proposal and not directly refute your competitors' arguments. This instinct probably stems from the correct belief that it won't help your cause to bad-mouth competitors or be negative. But there is a lot of territory between bad-mouthing and the most effective strategy—knowledgeably, fairly, and constructively refuting your competitors' claims.

When you know your competitors, it's a mistake to leave their arguments unanswered.

Blind Competition

Although refuting competing claims is the most effective way of dealing with competitors, it's not always possible. You may not know enough about your competitors' claims and supporting arguments, or you may have no competitive advantages. If you're applying for a job, you may know others are also applying, but it's unlikely you'll know who they are, much less anything about their qualifications.

In a blind competition, you should say nothing about competitors. No matter how intense the competition may be, nothing you say about competitors can help your case, or your perceived credibility and trustworthiness. And there is much you can say that will hurt you.

Knowledge Versus Good Judgment

If competitive information is available, take the time to learn about your competitors' proposals and the strengths and weaknesses in their supporting arguments and data. It's an investment that will pay off when you have competitors trying to get their way at your expense.

If you're a professional bidding against other professionals, you should know almost as much about your key competitors as you do about your own firm. If you're a manager vying for your company's limited resources, you should know not only why your proposal is good, but also why it's *better.* If you're a parent competing with forces outside the family for your child's values or behavior, you should be aware of the alternatives he's being offered and why they're the wrong ones.

But no matter how informed you may be about competitors, using what you know requires good judgment. Too much negative information, even when true, can appear unfair and unduly harsh. It can work against you the way negative political ads sometimes backfire on politicians. While you must refute your competitors' arguments, the preponderance of your case must still rest on how your proposal, standing on its own, meets your Prospect's needs.

It's especially important not to present unfounded beliefs as facts. If you *believe* your competitor is a dishonest, lying scoundrel, or that his products are shoddy, or that his service is the worst in the industry, or that your son's friends are lazy bums, these are not beliefs you can share with others unless your information is based on objective, verifiable facts. Remember, saying things you can't substantiate destroys your credibility.

Be sensitive to the possibility that your negative beliefs are incorrect exaggerations you may think are true, but that are in reality unproven opinions. Cohesive groups like families, teams, companies, and even entire countries form stereotypical, negative images of adversaries that are useful for team building, but that appear hostile, prejudicial, and unfair to outsiders, including your Prospects.

Gentle Persuasion Habit No. 20

Know your competitors. If possible, deal with their arguments head-on. If you don't know your competitors, ignore them entirely.

If you're a principled, well-mannered nice guy, there's no need to change just because you're up against a competitor. You can still attack head-on and help people do the right thing. Nice guys can finish first.

22

Persuasive Communication Made Easy

IT IS CLEAR ENOUGH THAT YOU ARE MAKING SOME
DISTINCTION IN WHAT YOU SAID, THAT THERE IS
SOME NICETY OF TERMINOLOGY IN YOUR WORDS. I
CAN'T QUITE FOLLOW YOU.

—*Flann O'Brien*

In the true Poet spirit, let's make persuasion as simple as possible. As it turns out, only two things really matter in persuasive communication: what's on your Prospects' minds while you're talking, and the way you choose to persuade them.

The Other Guy's Mind

When you're selling—talking, presenting, persuading, putting on the dog-and-pony show—it's too easy to focus inward, on what *you're* thinking and what *you're* going to say next. But you really need to know what your listener is thinking. Although you can seldom know exactly what someone else is thinking, you do know your listener will be in one of only four states of mind while you're talking. I call these four states Gone Fishing, Undecided, For You, and Against You.

Gone Fishing

In the Gone Fishing state of mind, your listener is not paying attention to what you're saying, not thinking through and processing the information you're presenting. Oh, sure, she's listening enough so she can carry on her side of the conversation without appearing rude or stupid, but her mind is elsewhere—on her next meeting, on her tennis game, on whether she'll have time to pick up the dog after work—her mind has "gone fishing."

If you're talking to your spouse or your kids and they don't seem to be paying attention, guess what. They're not. And as long as they're not paying attention, you're wasting good air by talking to them.

As we discussed in chapter 17, if you're talking to your Prospect while her brain has Gone Fishing, *you're not going to be persuasive no matter what you say or how you say it*. But the good news is that you can follow the advice in that chapter to avoid Talking Without Communicating. Just remember to first get people's attention by using their names and the pronoun *you*, and through stories and mystery.

Undecided

The good thing about the Gone Fishing mode is that you can always assume this is where the people you're talking to start out; if you work at it, it's not too hard to move them out of it. The Undecided state of mind is a little harder to spot and harder still to change. But if you don't change it, your chances of being persuasive are no better than fifty-fifty.

When your listener is in the Undecided mode, he's listening to what you're saying, but hasn't yet formed a clear mental picture of what it all really means. This happens when people don't know you or the subject you're presenting, and haven't had enough time to form opinions or biases.

Certainly people are Undecided when you meet them for

the first time and you're presenting them with a new idea. After shaking hands and making introductions, you begin talking, trying to make your case. Because your listener doesn't have an opinion on what you're talking about, instead of just listening to the facts, evidence, and logic you're presenting, he's trying to form a mental framework to help him sort out the information you're giving him. As long as your listener is Undecided, he's not so much thinking about what you're saying as about what he should think about what you're saying.

You're meeting with a prospective client for the first time. You begin by telling him the number of partners in your firm, the years you've been in business, that you have the best professionals in the industry, and that your firm prides itself on achieving high client satisfaction. If your listener knows nothing about you or your firm, you can bet his reaction to what you're telling him isn't, "Well, this is very useful information. It tells me this is the kind of firm I want to do business with." No. What your listener is thinking is more likely, "What does this all mean? Is this good, or is it just like most other firms? Can I trust what this person is telling me? Should I agree with this guy or not? Do I even care?"

Your listener is trying to create a mental picture in his mind about what you're telling him, a personal position for the idea you're presenting. This mental picture is the lens he'll use to view everything he hears about the idea, just as your personal position is the lens he uses to view information about you personally.

This process of creating a position for an idea at the same time he's listening to you talk about it for the first time is hard work. It distracts from the message you're trying to communicate. But, worse, if you haven't positioned what you're going to say before you say it, the conclusions your listener draws will be unpredictable.

You want to persuade your company's CEO, who has no background or interest in technology, to approve the purchase of an advanced order-processing system for your department. Although he doesn't personally know you or anything about the way your department runs, he's an intelligent, concerned executive and he's prepared to listen closely to what you have to say.

At first you may think this is exactly where you want him to be—listening to you with an open mind, thinking about what you're saying, and objectively processing the information to come to the conclusion you're leading him to. But the end result is too unpredictable. Let's see what can happen.

If your presentation follows tradition, you begin by providing background on your department, followed by a description of the system you want approved, followed by a presentation of the technology supporting it, and concluding with information on the vendor you've chosen.

But the CEO, with no mental frame of reference, doesn't know how to interpret the information you're giving him, so as you talk he works to develop one that helps him makes sense of what you're saying. Unfortunately, although he comes to the meeting with an open mind on your proposal, he also comes with a host of past experiences that may influence his thinking in ways you don't intend.

As you try to impress him with the features and benefits of your system, he wonders if the capabilities you're so enthusiastically describing mean it will be too expensive, or too difficult for his people to install and learn, or too risky for the company.

As you describe the product's cutting-edge technology, he's thinking about a conversation he had with a fellow board member who had a bad experience installing a complex system. So instead of being impressed, he's worrying that the technology will make the system less reliable.

Instead of using what you're saying as evidence to support the points you're trying to make, the CEO is trying to figure out if what you're saying is positive or negative for the company. But, even worse, left to his own devices, he's calling on random past experiences and attitudes to come to different conclusions from the ones you're trying to lead him to.

If your listener is Undecided, first change his state of mind to For You by using positioning statements we'll discuss next. If you're not sure your listener is Undecided, no problem. Once you're got your listener's attention, you can simply assume he's Undecided. There's no harm in beginning with the assumption that your listener is Undecided, even if he's already For You.

For You

The old cliché "preaching to the choir" expresses the simple idea that it's easy to persuade people who already believe what you want them to believe. Yet this intuitively obvious idea is the basis for persuasive communication. *If you only try to persuade people who are predisposed to believe what you want them to believe, you're far more likely to get your way.*

But how can you be sure everyone you need to persuade will be For You? Of course, it might be your good fortune that your listener's past experiences makes him positively biased toward what you're proposing. Great, because that means he's far more likely to interpret what you're saying in the positive light you intend, without a lot of extra work on your part. If your prospective client already thinks your firm is the best in the industry and you tell him about the advertising awards your creative department has won, he'll take this information as confirmation of his belief that your firm is tops. If he begins without a positive bias toward your firm, he may just wonder what winning creative advertising awards has to do with actually selling stuff.

If your listener doesn't start out in the For You state of mind, then put her there. Bias her so that she's predisposed to agree with you *before* you present each new idea. Then you're just changing the cliché from "preaching to the choir" to "preaching to the converted."

You can increase the chances your listener will be For You by using position statements. To get the CEO's approval for your department's new order-processing system, you might use the following series of positioning statements: "As you know, my department processes all the company's orders. As the company has grown, it has outgrown our order-processing system's ability to provide prompt service. If we don't upgrade the system now, by next year we won't be able to support the volume of orders the sales force is generating." You can now describe how your department works, or present statistics or comments from people in other departments, and the CEO will know what conclusion to draw, and why it's all relevant to him.

Moving on, you might introduce your next idea as follows: "Over the past three months I've personally studied all our options for upgrading the system. I've met with all the vendors and visited many of their customers. I know the technology each vendor uses, and how well the vendors support their customers in the real world." This is effective personal positioning. It positions you in the CEO's mind as exactly the kind of competent expert he wants to recommend a solution for the company.

Now you can introduce your recommendation with a positioning statement of this kind: "My recommendation is the best for the company, and is supported by all the people in my department and by both the sales and operations managers. The vendor has an excellent track record and the system is a low-risk solution that will support us for the foreseeable future." This tells the CEO how he should think about the proposal you're about to make.

These positioning statements serve as clear mental outlines the CEO can use to sort and organize the ideas and information you give him. Unless he's prejudiced against you or your proposal for some reason, he'll listen to what you say in the light of these positioning statements. If he was Undecided, there's a good change you'll have made him For You—biased him to accept you, your ideas, and your entire proposal.

Gentle Persuasion Habit No. 21

To help people understand and agree with you, use positioning statements to introduce each new idea.

Against You

Unfortunately there are times when life deals you a tough hand and you face someone who's biased against you or what you're proposing. Maybe a competitor has already won your Prospect over, or past experiences have caused him to form strong beliefs that don't support you. Just as "Ford guys" can't hear anything good about Chevies, it may be that your teenager's friends have convinced him all parents are losers, or your boss may believe the Apple computers you're proposing aren't suitable for business computing.

When your listener is against you for some reason, it doesn't matter that he's paying attention to what you're saying. He starts out disagreeing with you, and he'll use what you're saying to prove you're wrong.

Let's go back to the CEO and the new order-processing system you're trying to get him to approve. You don't know it, but his daughter works for a company that sells a competing system you've evaluated and rejected. The CEO's daughter, seeing that you stand in the way of a sale, has told her father you're not exactly the brightest bulb in the hardware store. So you walk into the meeting with a big smile, a firm handshake, and a big zero tattooed on your forehead, which you don't see, but the CEO does.

In the CEO's mind you're not competent, a serious problem

for any persuader. He starts out biased against you and your recommendation, and even if you introduce each idea with an effective positioning statement, he'll discount most of what you say.

If his daughter works for a larger, better established company than the one you're recommending, he'll believe small companies are too risky for large companies like his to do business with. If she works for a small startup and you're recommending a well-established company, he'll believe big companies are too mired in old technology and bureaucracy to meet the needs of companies like his.

He'll evaluate everything you say in the light of his negative bias. You'll be mentally scratching your head, wondering why you can't get to first base.

Don't think you can cure this negative bias just by providing compelling information that can only lead in the direction you're heading. Everything in life can be interpreted in different ways. People can take your Harvard diploma as evidence either that you're intelligent or that you're an elitist. That you worked for a big company for ten years may make you seem loyal and stable to some, and risk-averse to others. That you have a family may make you look like a responsible adult to some people, or too likely to be distracted from your work to others.

The power of prejudice is so strong that it, even more than what you say, often determines the conclusion your listener arrives at.

Winning Against Prejudice

So there you are, facing a boss, child, spouse, client, or someone else who starts out mentally set against you or what you're about to propose. Maybe it's your fault, maybe not.

Your boss's opinion of you may be low because you didn't go to the "right" schools; your teenager thinks you're a dweeb because he's under the influence of his peers; your spouse wants nothing to do with spending the holidays duck hunting because last year's bass-fishing vacation was a disaster; and your client has lost confidence in you now that he's behind bars.

Whether it's possible to win people over to your point of view when they start out Against You or what you're proposing depends on the strength of the negative bias and your approach. Persuasion studies show that to persuade people who start out believing something different from what you want them to believe, you must

1. get their attention;
2. motivate them to think about what you're saying;
3. be credible;
4. not be perceived to have such a strong interest in the position you're taking that it will cause you to recommend something that's good for you but not for them;
5. present logical reasons for the inconsistencies between their beliefs and experiences and what you're asking them to believe;
6. present *strong* proof that what you're saying is true.

Let's say you're a woman interviewing for a job with someone you strongly suspect doesn't think women can make the sacrifices necessary to succeed in business. Sure, you can begin by selling yourself, telling vivid stories, and giving "test drives" that give your interviewer a personal experience of working with you. This is the approach that Alice, the systems consultant we talked about in the "Vivid Storytelling" section of chapter 20, used successfully.

This strategy worked well for her, because her gender was a relatively minor concern compared with all the legitimate buying anxieties. But if you believe the negative bias is serious business, you should deal with it up front.

In this example, I don't want to oversimplify the difficulty women and minorities have in overcoming intransigent prejudice. While some people can be won over, others simply can't. The assumption here is that we're not dealing with hard-core bigotry.

As always, the first job is to capture your listener's attention and give him a reason to think about what you're saying. This is especially important with Prospects who start out Against You, because people with a negative bias tend to tune out what they don't want to hear.

There are any number of ways to get this interviewer's attention, but one possibility is: "I know your company has an excellent reputation for hiring women. But I also understand you may be concerned that I may not be able to travel or otherwise work the hours necessary to do what you need me to do in this job." You must say this in a positive, nonthreatening way, but however you say it, it's sure to capture your interviewer's attention and motivate him to listen to you.

You can then align your interviewer's needs with yours: "Believe me, I wouldn't take a job where I couldn't do everything you needed me to do to be successful. It doesn't do either of us any good if the job requires me to travel or work weekends and for some reason I can't."

The next step is to give credible proof that the negative beliefs you suspect the interviewer holds are not true: "I know travel is an important part of the job. Fortunately, travel is not a problem for me. In my last job I spent 40 percent of my time on the road. At one point I spent an entire month in Europe closing an important sale at the end of our fiscal year."

Notice that up to this point you haven't given the interviewer a single reason for hiring you. You haven't talked about your past experience or education, or discussed your management style. None of the standard stuff of job interviews. You may, in fact, be entirely unqualified for the job. But assuming you're not talking to a hopeless Neanderthal, you've probably moved your interviewer from being Against You to being For You. Now you're ready to begin the real interview, ready to prove, tell vivid stories, and give test drives, more than confident your persuasion efforts will be listened to, believed, and received positively.

If your interviewer had started out For You, your job would have been much easier; you would only have had to worry about the first three of the six steps. But you are where you are, and you must carefully follow the six steps above to try to turn things around. Maybe you'll be successful with this interviewer, but in other situations, no matter how well you prepare and how eloquently and logically you make your case, there's still a good chance you'll fail when someone starts out Against You.

If the boss's fraternity brother is in line for the promotion you're shooting for, you may be facing an impossible sale. If your musician son really hates business, cubicles, and sensible shoes, persuading him to join you in your accounting practice may be a futile exercise, no matter how well you prepare your arguments. But you follow the six-step formula above and give it your best shot. If you succeed, great. If you fail, move on without destroying the relationship between you and your Prospect. Time passes and things change, and if you maintain good relationships, who knows what the future will bring?

The Man Behind the Curtain

The tricky thing about positioning new ideas is that your personal position can overshadow, for better or for worse, the position you're trying to create for your ideas. If you have a negative position in your listeners' minds—say they don't think you're competent, trustworthy, or someone who puts their interests first—it may be impossible for you to position your ideas so they will be in the For You mind-set. On the other hand, if you have a strongly positive personal position, you'll find it easy to position your ideas.

My son attended boarding school for the first time in the seventh grade and was doing well, so I was eager for him to continue. He was happy at the school, but sometimes missed the easier-going atmosphere of our local schools, and wasn't sure he wanted to continue at boarding school in the eighth grade.

Fortunately my son knows that, when it comes to his education, I'm competent, trustworthy, and think only of his best interests. I have a strong positive personal position.

I was able to positively position the idea that he stay in his current school by reminding him that his decision to attend the school helped him academically more than all the other efforts he and we had made. The new school allowed him to go from average grades to honors, to participate in serious competitive sports that weren't available at the local schools, and to make many new friends. Although he was initially undecided, after a ten-minute conversation he decided he should stay in the same school at least through the eighth grade.

I was persuasive because I have a strong personal position with my son. He allowed me to be persuasive.

But I have a negative personal position in my daughter's mind when it comes to vacations, especially vacations involving bicycles. She has seen me drag her and our family and friends to remote corners of the country to mountain-bike, simply because I enjoy it. While I certainly hope everyone else enjoys it also, I have to concede she's right in believing that that's not my overriding concern. Good father or not, she knows I'm not putting her needs first when it comes to anything having to do with bicycles. As a result, there's nothing I can say to positively position the idea of a mountain-biking vacation. The conversation goes downhill from my first words.

As in *The Wizard of Oz*, no one ignores the man behind the curtain—in this case, the person positioning the ideas. When it comes to your personal position, you reap what you sow.

The Communications Matrix

Half the secret of persuasive communication is to be sure your listeners are For You before you try to persuade them of anything. The second half has to do with how you make your case, how you present the ideas and conclusions you want your listeners to agree with.

In Step 3 we reviewed four different ways to go about persuading your Prospect—telling, proving, using vivid images through the use of stories, and providing personal experiences through test drives. We can now combine those two dimensions of communications—what the listener is thinking and how you're presenting—to create a model of persuasive communication. The model is illustrated below.

THE COMMUNICATIONS MATRIX

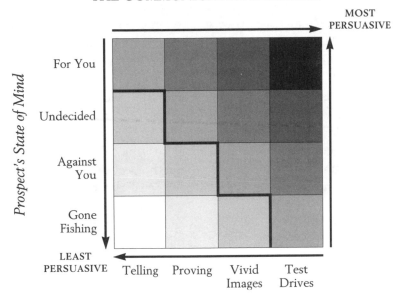

How You're Communicating

The farther you move toward the upper right-hand corner of this matrix, the more likely it is you'll have a persuasive conversation with your listener. In the extreme upper right, you've positioned yourself so your Prospect has a mind-set that makes him positively biased toward your proposition, and you're providing him with personal experiences though test drives. Your success is nearly assured.

At the other extreme—the lower left—you're talking, but the person you're talking to isn't listening. Even worse, you're "telling," trying to persuade without providing strong proof, vivid images, or personal experiences. Your failure is nearly assured.

As you move from the lower left to the upper right, your chances of being persuasive increase, which is represented by the gradations of shading. So your objective is to get from wherever you start out to as close to the upper right corner as possible.

The interesting question is whether you should first move to the right or first move upward. The temptation is to first move to the right because you're entirely in control of where you are on the horizontal axis. It's you and you alone who can decide whether to tell, prove, provide vivid images, or give test drives. It's your listener, on the other hand, who decides where you sit on the vertical scale. Because he's the one who's Gone Fishing, Against You, Undecided, or For You, it seems as if you have less control over your vertical position.

So, instinctively, you might believe the best persuasion strategy is to move to the right. But most of the time you'd be wrong.

Let's say you begin on the bottom of the matrix with your listener not really paying attention. The matrix shows you'll be slightly more persuasive if you provide vivid images or give test drives, but only because these approaches might gain your listener's attention. You'll communicate far more persuasively if you gain your listener's attention *before* you begin to persuade. If your listener isn't paying close attention to what you're about to say, if he doesn't believe that what you're about to say is going to be important to him, if he's not more interested in what you're about to say in the next minute or so than in anything else that may be on his mind at the moment, use the techniques in chapter 17 to gain his attention and move him upward on the matrix.

If you begin with your listener Against You, you might conceivably persuade her if you move to the right. But you're far more likely to be successful if you can first change your listener's negative bias. So before you begin presenting your point of view, follow the six steps presented earlier in this chapter. Motivate your listener to pay attention and think about what you're saying. Be credible, and make it clear that you and your listener share common interests and needs. Present logical reasons why their beliefs may not be true, and present strong proof to support your claims.

Similarly, if your listener is Undecided, use positioning statements to move to the For You part of the matrix before launching into the heart of your persuasive presentation.

The Communications Matrix shows a heavy line separating the lower left of the matrix from the upper right. If you find yourself below the line, you're almost certainly Talking Without Communicating. If you're above the line, great, but try to get as far above it as possible, preferably in the For You section, before you begin persuading. Finally, when you're happy with where you are with your listener and it's time to begin persuading, your strategy should rely mostly on providing personal experiences though vivid stories and test drives.

That's all there is to it.

23

The Bottom Line

WHY DO MEN DELIGHT IN WORK? FUNDAMENTALLY,
I SUPPOSE, BECAUSE THERE IS A SENSE OF RELIEF AND
PLEASURE IN GETTING SOMETHING DONE—A KIND
OF SATISFACTION NOT UNLIKE THAT WHICH A HEN
ENJOYS ON LAYING AN EGG.

—*H. L. Mencken*

Of the hundreds, perhaps thousands, of persuasion tactics accumulated over decades of selling and persuading, we've isolated the following twenty-one that support an ethical Three-Step Plan for winning the minds and hearts of the people you care about.

STEP 1: FULFILL PEOPLE'S PERSONAL NEEDS

1. Make people feel like winners. Never turn issues into win-lose contests. In the long run, you lose every contest of wills.
2. Don't underestimate people's need for security, predictability, and low risk. Make your proposals as risk-free as possible.
3. Remember that the people you're trying to persuade care about what others think. You won't get your way if what you're asking doesn't meet with the approval of others.
4. Discipline yourself to think and talk more about people's personal needs and less about their situational needs.

5. Let the other guy talk first. Always begin by asking questions and listening—really listening. Before you try to persuade people, you must understand people's personal needs and how what you're proposing might fulfill them.

6. Be prepared to deal with people's five buying anxieties as they get closer to making a decision.
   - "But what about the options I'm giving up?"
   - "Am I making a mistake by agreeing with you?"
   - "How will I explain my decision to others?"
   - "Am I going to come out of this a loser?"
   - "Is this going to cost me too much?"

7. Be "easy-to"—easy-to-buy, easy-to-deal-with, easy-to-do-business-with, and easy-to-live-with.

8. Stay in sync with people's natural buying process. Talk about what they're prepared to listen to.

STEP 2: BE CREDIBLE

9. Become competent. Know your stuff, do your homework, learn, and demonstrate your competence. If you can't become an expert, team up with one.

10. Be trustworthy. Be scrupulously and consistently honest, fair, and positive.

11. Put the personal needs of others first, and then align your needs with theirs.

12. Don't worry about body language, being liked, being similar to others, or making an outstanding first impression. If you're competent, trustworthy, and put other people's interests first, you can just be yourself.

13. Key the way you dress to the way others dress, but always dress in a way that's consistent with your message.

STEP 3: COMMUNICATE PERSUASIVELY

14. Talk to people in terms of *their* interests and needs, not in terms of *your* interests and needs.

15. Get people's attention before you talk.

16. Position yourself in a way that's succinct, unambiguous,

distinctive, and relevant. Always act consistently with your personal position.

17. Telling isn't selling. Collect evidence and references, and weave them into a credible, substantiating story that proves your claims.

18. To persuade people who don't know you or to sell new ideas, give a test drive.

19. With everyone, always keep your promises, do what you say you're going to do, and make them happy they let you get your way.

20. Know your competitors. If possible, deal with their arguments head-on. If you don't know your competitors, ignore them entirely.

21. To help people understand and agree with you, use positioning statements to introduce each new idea.

These twenty-one Gentle Persuasion Habits will help you put the Three-Step Plan into practice. Practice and live the Three-Step Plan if you must sell yourself, your ideas, or your services to achieve your potential. You'll communicate more effectively, and you'll get your way in everyday life. You'll win the minds and hearts of the people you care about, and you'll do it without compromising your principles or doing stuff you hate.

And that's a good thing.

Afterword

I'M AS PURE AS THE DRIVEN SLUSH.

—*Tallulah Bankhead*

There's an episode of *I Love Lucy* in which Lucy writes a novel. The only problem is that the characters are all thinly disguised people from her real life—Fred, Ethel, Ricky, and herself. Worse still, with the exception of Lucy, everybody comes off so poorly that they all become angry at her. She faces the prospect of having all the most important people in her life turn against her.

I could see myself in the same situation if I wasn't careful. For this reason, with the exception of my immediate family, I've tried to disguise the people and particulars in most of the examples and stories I've used in the book. Of course I've changed names, but with Lucy's experience in mind, I've done more. I've randomly changed people's genders, ages, and professions. I've changed the settings and circumstances so the characters are less recognizable. In some cases I've even combined several personal experiences into a single experience that illustrates a single point.

There are two messages here. The first is that the stories and examples in the book are true, though sometimes heavily camouflaged. The second is that if you're a friend or colleague and you think you recognize yourself in a story, you're probably wrong. You're the one in the story that doesn't sound anything like you.

I tried to treat my wife and children kindly, never showing them in an unfavorable light. They read everything that includes them before publication, and had ample opportunity to protest. In the case of my children, I hope that they'll judge me no more harshly for their treatment in this book than they do when I show people their baby pictures—sort of as typical family stuff you've got to expect from parents. Part of the normal cost of growing up.

Although it may be confusing at times, I only have two children, a girl and a boy. When I refer to their ages in the book, it's their ages at the time of the incident I'm describing. So my six-year-old, eleven-year-old, and twelve-year-old sons are all the same son.

Incidentally, Lucy did get her novel published. A publisher bought it as an example of how not to write a novel.

Thank You

Creators, whether they're parents, artists, or writers, fall in love with their creations. We just can't look at them dispassionately and see them as others see them. An ugly baby is beautiful to its parents; I'm sure that whoever paints all those Elvises on black velvet believes the paintings are true art; and I know writers read their own stuff the way a gourmet savors a great dish. Except that the writer does it without a sense of taste.

With writers, this shortcoming is not merely ego. It's overfamiliarity wrought by overexposure, the result of having to reread what we've written a hundred times. We quickly become word-blind, unable to distinguish between what's in our minds and what's on paper, between what we've meant to say and what we've said, between what we think is clear, interesting, and useful, and what's a crashing bore. It's a disease with only one cure: You've got to get someone else to read your stuff.

If you've never had to read the early drafts of a full-length work, you can never fully appreciate how much of a sacrifice this is, and how much it means to an author. Fortunately, I have friends and colleagues who made the sacrifice and read the book as I wrote it, some in many drafts, and provided comments that were not simply helpful, but essential.

I especially thank Laureen Bedell and Michael Mills of Davis Polk and Wardwell for not just volunteering to read nearly every draft, but almost demanding to. They'd return drafts with detailed comments and observations in the margins. They'd spend hours talking about what was right and wrong.

As attorneys who must persuade others as part of their everyday lives, their comments were particularly relevant. They did so much work and were so helpful that I actually began feeling guilty and stopped sending them drafts despite their requests for the latest versions. There's only so much torture anyone should endure. Before long, Amnesty International would have intervened.

Jay Gaines, founder and CEO of the New York City executive search firm Jay Gaines & Company; Vivek Wadhwa, founder and CEO of Relativity Software; and Irene Wong, vice president of Human Resources at the Power Systems division of Invensys, all read very early drafts. These are senior executives who must persuade people within and outside their organizations every day. Their honest and insightful comments and observations were so valuable that I entirely changed the structure and tone of the book. I doubt they'll recognize the final work. Or at least I hope they don't.

Tom Dungan, president of Management Concepts; Srini Vasan, cofounder and president of Letteau Ltd.; and Barbara Beech of Management Concepts all read middle drafts and helped me make midcourse corrections. Susan Luth, Wendy Grammas, and John Ryan read and commented on later drafts.

I would especially like to thank John Engles, cofounder of Letteau Ltd., for being the first to give me the opportunity to apply the ideas of the book in a formal selling and business environment, and my editor, Bob Mecoy of Crown Books, for the insights that made the book clearer and more interesting.

Finally, I thank my wife, Deborah, who read every word of every draft of this book, just as she read every work of every draft of my first book. As a lawyer, businessperson, parent, and woman, she contributed a uniquely insightful perspective. As an editor, she reduced the time required to complete the book by half and helped me find the book's voice. As a source of confidence, support, companionship, and good humor, she increased the fun of the project twofold and my joy of living tenfold.

Index

About the Author

WHAT REALLY KNOCKS ME OUT IS A BOOK THAT,
WHEN YOU'RE ALL DONE READING IT, YOU WISH THE
AUTHOR THAT WROTE IT WAS A TERRIFIC FRIEND OF
YOURS AND YOU COULD CALL HIM UP ON THE
PHONE WHENEVER YOU FELT LIKE IT.

—*J. D. Salinger*

Gene Bedell is founder and chairman of Tenzing L.L.C., a company whose mission is to help people and organizations achieve their potential. He can be reached at his company's offices in Great Falls, Virginia, at (703) 759-3606, or by e-mail at gene@tenzingLLC.com.

If you've found the advice in this book useful in your business, professional, or everyday life, he'd appreciate hearing about it by e-mail or regular mail. His postal address is Tenzing L.L.C., P.O. Box 173, Great Falls, VA 22066.